The Jaycee Diaries

THROUGH THE EYES OF A CHILD

K.C. Green

authorHOUSE®

AuthorHouse™ LLC
1663 Liberty Drive
Bloomington, IN 47403
www.authorhouse.com
Phone: 1-800-839-8640

Published by AuthorHouse   07/14/2014

ISBN: 978-1-4969-2641-8 (sc)
ISBN: 978-1-4969-2642-5 (e)

You know when you know. For example, when you go to an awesome restaurant and order the most gigantic piece of home made layered fudge cake, or, even better, cherry cheesecake, which you would never order on any regular day because of all the calories, and the waiter brings it to your table and can barely set it down before you dive in face first. Well, this is that kind of story about a sweet young child. It might make you laugh, or cry, or think about how relatable it is, or not. Much like the dessert, one bite just isn't enough; if you're ordering something really good, you want to commit to the very end. Right?

Middeltown Rhode Island, 1982

I was born to married parents; Victor Mac Googliano (yeah, I know, a real mouthful!) and Jean Stefa Phillis. Oh, did I mention that I was born on the Eve of Christmas? I always heard people say "Oh, how unlucky that must have been", but not me. I felt that it was the one day of the year that was actually mine, and even better, mine to share. Now, if it had been Christmas Day, well, that's a different story. I mean, who would want to eat birthday cake on Christmas? People also would say that my birthday stinks because I must get a raw deal on gifts, but, no, that's not the case at all. The fact that my whole family received gifts on my birthday really brought me great joy. I felt like no one got left out.

My mother worked at the shipyard down the road, and my father did some assembly work on the line there as well. That's how they met, of course; work. We lived at 6 Mariam Court up a very small rocky drive with a couple of other houses in the back and a small cul-de-sac in front of the driveway. It was a three bedroom with a living room, kitchen, one and a half bathroom and a decent sized yard with a tire swing that hung from the branch of a huge oak tree. We had a small basement that was very musty. It almost reminded me of the soggy moss smell that grew from the earth. The bottom line; it was a place that kept us warm, but a home? Not so much. My ma worked a ton, as well as my Father, so for a lot of my younger childhood we were left with various babysitters- mostly younger high school kids- while my parents worked and went out. My real saving grace was my grandmother- the other Jean. Jean Stefa Phillis, of course. She was a heavy set, salt-and-pepper-haired woman who liked to cook, clean, and bitch about life. (And being married to my grandfather, who wouldn't?) Frank (well, Franklin) Peter Phillis (my grandmother would holler his name), was a tall, balding WWII veteran with many deep war scars to hide. Sometimes, though, they were not as easily hidden as he would have liked. Once he was at a gas station by his camp when someone threw a bomb and the gas station exploded around him. Wow, was he lucky. All that really happened was his right nipple was blown up, but for some unknown reason he left it there to dangle down his breast. I also think that on that side he went slightly deaf, which is why my grandmother was a pro at yelling, "Frank!"

I also have an older brother. He was a year and a half older than me. Erick Mac was his name, and being a Bozo was his game. Let's put it this way; he's always been... I'm struggling to even find a word to describe the type of person my brother is, and, I guess this is going to sound horrible, but dumb black lab would probably be best. The kind that runs out into traffic, even though there's a good possibility of getting hit or badly injured. I saw that happen once with a lab that my parents had, the stupid dog was lucky to be alive. I could have choked that thing! My point is, my brother didn't know any better, and I wasn't really sure that he ever would. He looked a lot like my mother; dirty blonde hair, light, sky-blue eyes- overall, a good looking Polish kid. My mother was Polish, her mother was one hundred percent Polish and she spoke it too! Boy, did I learn the term Stubborn Polack quick! However, our father was one hundred percent Italian, and he looked it, too! It was him. His fathers name was Tony, and his father before that, and so on. I looked like my father, the complete opposite of my mother and brother, with dark brown hair, deep blue eyes, and more of an olive skin tone; I was not really Polish looking one bit. So, that made it an even split from our parents.

Probably the last memory I have of my mother and father that year was when we were at the shipyard down the road from our house where mom works. We were there to watch the annual fireworks display, which we had done every year. My brother and I were so happy to be there. It was such a nice day- how could we not be excited? We always got to sit in the back of my father's old, red, Ford pickup truck. I can remember looking up at the dark sky that showed thousands of gold, sparkling stars. Oh, they were so wonderful! There were super long rows of parked cars. The rows went on for miles and filled the whole lot. I saw every car color you could think of that night. People were sitting in their beach chairs, just waiting for the glitz and glam of the sky to spark, and then it happened. One of my ding-dong parents locked the keys in the cab. They were quick to blame each other. My brother and I were already in the back of the pickup, so we were out of the way, but we could hear the chaos our parents were making and decided to ignore them. I would say that my first real memory came that day, and has stayed with me forever after. During my parent's lack of communication, I was snatched! I was taken right out of the pickup truck! He was a large, tall, and scary black man. I remember my brother's face as he looked up at me. It was kind of a helpless, silent scream of terror, but mostly a look of shock in those blue five-year-old eyes, so innocent. As my two piggy tales flapped in the wind, I might have realized that I may not ever see my parents again, and how much I would miss them. We were now running fast as he carried me. I began to shake and cry. He was going so fast, and I was being jiggled around like a garbage bag in a dumpster. He took no care with me at all, and his force was too rough for me. We flew. I can still picture the blurred color of cars, and then a loud boom and a final thud, and I was out as cold as ice. I awoke to the sound of loud fireworks and looked up into the sky to see the most amazing ruby red firework burst into the stars. My parents had already started giving me a thousand hugs and kisses. They had a look of sorrow and I knew it had been the most awful experience they had ever had, and me as well! I really just liked the fact that they were happy again, and that they had me. Some say it was luck and others say it was fate, but I think God had other plans for my life that day. Apparently there was an older couple that had seen the entire thing go down, right from my knucklehead parents locking the keys in the damn car! Being good citizens of our local town, they sprung into action and screamed at the man to "drop the girl now!" The elderly gentleman even started after us at one point. I was so thankful to them, and I bashfully gave them a wave goodbye that night.

September, 1986

My parents were more on edge than ever that year. My brother and I each had a regular birthday with them, but we could always feel something more. They worked like dogs, and my Father was becoming less and less involved with us kids, being too busy to make any time for us. We understood too well that working parents were too tired for play and fun; it wasn't even an option for us. We hadn't even visited the local park in at least a month's time. Our sitters would mostly watch television while we played in our rooms alone. My room was a place that became all too familiar to me, and I was getting stir crazy. My Grandmother started to step in and offer to take me more, and I was thrilled to be with her. We were starting to become more like buddies who would shop, eat and swim all day. She really was my most favorite person in the whole world at the time. She gave me the most of her time, and that's all I could have asked.

Her name was Pauletta. Yeah, I know, the worst name I think anyone could be given. I hated it when I heard my mom speak it. She was the reason he had cheated. After my mom got laid off from her job at the shipyard, she went to the local Caldor's. My God, it was the first super store in my town. I'll never forget that sign, so high up. Well, she worked there for a short time, and made a friend. For my mom to bring a friend home was a big deal; she worked so much that she usually never found the time. Pauletta came around a few times, and then when she met my father she came around a lot more. It wasn't long after that he left my mother. My mom always told me how ugly he became when he got caught in a lie. I guess he even held a knife to her head saying not to "dare take the kids away". Yeah, that's pretty ugly if you ask me. There was a filing for divorce shortly after. My mother didn't play, and she knew things would get ugly and that they were about to go from bad to worse.

Mothers resort was what can sometimes be heartbreaks best friend; the bottle. The bar down the road called "The Sea Swirl" was quickly becoming her most popular setting. Conveniently, it was located at the end of our driveway and to the left. I will always remember the sea green seahorse on the sign that stood tall to the left of the bar. You could tell that all of the shipyard workers and the locals found it to be a most convenient spot, as they would flood the place day in and day out. I always saw them from the car as we drove by. It was a fixture on my road. I'm not sure if hate would best describe how I felt about that bar. I think jealousy was what I really felt. It stole my time with her away. There was too much lost time. My mom eventually started bringing home a few randoms here and there while the nasty divorce went on. The types of men who came through could have cared less if my brother and I were in the next room or not; they were there for one thing and one thing only.

Later that year there were two things that happened as my fifth birthday grew near. One was that the divorce was finalized and the second was that one of the men that my mother brought home never left. A sailor and his friend had passed out in our living room. I was startled and confused, and, being almost five, I felt that it was my job to protect my mother and brother from these intruders. So, I quietly snuck into the kitchen and grabbed the sharpest kitchen knife I could find. Bending over one of the men, studying his face and waiting for him to make a move was not my smartest choice, because he awoke, screaming. I was waving the knife around in his face and shaking, and he backed away with a really scared look in his eyes. He shouted for my mother and she came out fast, rushing at me and yelling "Jaycee, what in the hell is wrong with you?!" My reply was only tears. She explained that her "friends" had had too much to drink and she had invited them to stay over the night. *Geez, Ma, how considerate of you...* I thought. Well, one of the guys left that morning, but the other never did. His name was Theo; Theodore, actually, but after he was born everyone called him Theo. His mother wanted his name to be a stand out, so she chose to name him after our nations youngest president, Theodore Roosevelt. The truth is, I had no clue what to call him, or maybe I just didn't care. He had dark, feathery hair with a part right down the middle, and a heavier set demeanor. He knew that she had the baggage of kids and a nasty divorce on her hands, and yet that never swayed his decision of how he felt for her one bit. He pursued her, and she pursued him. The idea of becoming a Navy wife was her newest obsession, and having been laid off, what choice did she have? Soon a quickie wedding was in the works, so it was time for me to accept that any kind of parental reunion was never, ever going to happen. Change was always a hard thing for me to swallow, but I should have been used to it by now, since it happened all too often in my house.

Theo helped throw my fifth birthday party that year, and my whole family came to the house. I was pretty sure it was the perfect way for my mother to make his introduction into the family, and I'm also pretty sure that they couldn't have cared less that I was digging around in the medicine cabinet looking for a Band-Aid because I had scraped my knee outside. Well, leave it to me to dump an entire bottle of orange-reddish liquid down my beautiful, white birthday dress! When my mom found me, she knew that I was upset and never once yelled in anger, and in return I had better behavior for the rest of the party. I even got a bike, so I thought that maybe five would be all right.

Summer, 1987

The battle that my mother had fought against my father, Victor, was over and she won. She got everything that she could get, including money for child support, which he was not happy about; the last thing that he wanted to do was to give her a dime! He fought hard for custody of us, and he lost hard too. He ended up with only visitation rights every other weekend. He should have known; it was a women's state, after all. In her eyes, though, that would never be enough to cover the pain she and us kids had suffered, and believe you me, we would never hear the end of it either. Ever. Now it was time for the next chapter, though. I didn't think there would ever be a good kind of closure for them. There were too many bitter years ahead for the two of them, I knew that all too well. Boy, did they hate each other, and they didn't plan to hide it, either. I wanted to tell myself that things would get better after that, but I think a war was just beginning, one much bigger than me or my brother were prepared to handle. Mom had to wait a few weeks before she could get a cent from my father because as it turned out, he was trying to get disability from supposedly being very badly injured on the job at the shipyard. It was kind of strange, though, because I had never once seen him in any kind of pain, as far as I could remember. I always assumed that it must have been internal. Well, ma had to find a way to dig us out of this financial hole that we were in. It got pretty bad. We never had money for anything. Erick and I would rummage through the cupboards for anything to eat, and most of the time we came up empty handed. We would just glance sorry looks at each other, because we always had hope. I tried to make boxed macaroni and cheese once, but since I could barely read, this proved to be more of a challenge than I had hoped. Yup, everything got dumped into a giant, red mixing bowl and whisked around in cheesy, sloppy, clumpy, soupy orange circles in hopes that it would cook so I could try to feed Erick's hunger pains. Well, not only was it an epic fail, an even lower blow came to my heart. Theo walked up and caught me dumping the orange, rock hard mess in the back yard and unhappy does not even begin to describe the look I received. He screamed, and it made my whole body quiver. Not because I was in trouble- I knew the risk the second I had opened the box- but because I had never had a grown man use such a threatening tone with me before. He shouted that I was being wasteful, and that next time there would be consequences for such behavior. So, it was back to grape jelly and cheese on hot dog rolls for Erick (his idea, not mine) and nothing for me. That was the first time in my life that I felt truly angry.

The day of my mothers wedding, my grandmother decided it would be best to chop all of my hair off, and it probably wouldn't have been so bad if I didn't look like a five year old little boy. My mother freaked. I was no longer the little piggy-tailed haired girl she had always known. She truly hated it, and I was sad not only because she hated the new do, but because I did too. She was not alone, but her reaction of throwing a huge fit was like rubbing salt onto an open wound. I was not exactly sure why my grandmother did it, and the fact that she did it on this particular day was puzzling. Was this her way of showing my mother that she was stepping up in my life, or was this her way of getting even because she knew another wrong marriage choice was about to go down? Much of their relationship was spent bickering about my mother's wrongdoings, and to my grandmother there was never any shame in exposing her mistakes, no matter the time or the place.

There really wasn't much time to drag out the argument though, because the time quickly drew near for us to take our places. Since there was very little money to be spent on a big wedding, they made do with the best they had, and had a small wedding in the backyard. My mother looked pretty in her tan and white floral pantsuit. I knew that it was a smart choice for her, because she never had been a dress type of person. I liked it. Theo wore white slacks and a very nice Polo shirt. I liked his attire as well. Everyone looked better than me that day. I officially had the worst haircut on the earth, and my clothes looked beyond dorky; a white, button up, short sleeved, collared Polo, shorts with an odd floral pattern, and beat up, dirty looking tennis shoes. I was starting to really feel like the family misfit, and was so embarrassed as I stood to the right of my mother.

The glances that were exchanged between the two Jeans that day were surely evil. They had a way of letting each other know exactly how they felt without saying a word. But I knew. I knew how everyone felt that day. My grandfather hated Theo, and in no way did he intend to hide it. Even I saw the tension they felt, however being the good parents they were they managed to put on brave faces, which in my family was not easy to do. I was proud of them, and like it or not, I had just gotten a new step-dad.

As the wedding went on, I got to play with my cousins Keegan, Alexander and Dane, which was rare because it was obvious that our mothers were two sisters who did not get along. I liked my cousins, but I think that they felt a bit standoffish since we were practically strangers. They had always had better clothes, a better house, and they even had horses. I always felt jealous of how much they had, and I'm pretty sure that's why my mother was so bitter toward her sister Dinah. It made sense to me, anyway. Later, at the food table I met a man who was older; probably about seventy or so. His name was Lennon Kindsay, and he was a tall, grey-haired man who seemed to have a clean sense of style in black slacks and a button down long-sleeved shirt under a V-neck sweater. I thought that this was a strange outfit, since it was a summer wedding. He shook my hand and said that he was my neighbor, and then he told me that he was very happy for my mother because he never liked my father one bit, and it was nice to see him gone. Ok, I was offended! Who the hell was he to even mention my father on such a day. What an unkind person. I didn't want to be anywhere near him.

My parents never took a honeymoon, but later that year we did end up taking our first family vacation. My stepfather had family in Pennsylvania, so we packed up our wagon and we were on the road. I wasn't particularly happy about a three and a half hour car ride, but when we got there it was well worth it. Theo's parents were divorced a long time ago, so it was his father and stepmothers house that we were going to. They had such a great welcome for us. Everybody was out in front, waiting and waving as we drove up to the house. It made me smile, and I waved in return. They gave us all hugs and invited us in to a spread of breads, meats and cheeses. They had made everything, and I was so hungry. We had only stopped twice to pee. There was one meat in particular that I would never forget. It was one of the best tasting meats that I had ever eaten in my life. It was a salty ring of delicious smoked sausage, and it made my mouth water to even think about it after that day. It was called ring bologna, and I loved it! After we ate and got acquainted with everyone, we were free to explore. The house was huge, and it had the most amazing view of Amston Lake. I loved how they had an enclosed porch so that you could view the lake at any time of day without being eaten alive. The porch was my favorite part of that sweet lake house. Later that day we walked and swam and drove around the lake. It was such a beauty of nature, and I felt like all of the problems of my past were fading away as my new memories were being made. My biggest worry right now was getting bitten by a snapping turtle. It was nice to have Erick out of my hair, too! Theo had a much younger half brother who was still in high school, so my brother took to him, which was great. Well, for me at least. I popped in to say hi, and they were hitting it off perfectly. He even had a tidy room with the bed nicely made, a boom box stereo in the corner, and a pile of homework placed nicely on top. I couldn't believe it. That was when I realized that not all boys were slobs!

The next day we drove a few towns over to meet more of Theo's lovely family. He had an older brother who was married with kids, as well as aunts, uncles, and the sweetest ninety-year-old grandmother, Gram Golden. And she was golden! I could see and feel it all around her. I thought of her as someone who was wise and beautiful. Her white hair was even an almost golden color. I loved being near her. I had no idea that when I went to Pennsylvania that year that I would fall in love with the family of a man that I barely knew. I felt my heart grow bigger while I was there with his family on that vacation.

Later That Year

Theo had been gone to sea for about six months now, and my mother was growing restless, as were we. She had to work a ton and we were running really short on cash. The refrigerator showed it; we were like mice looking for crumbs. We hadn't been on any more trips, so it was a sad time for us. I could tell that she really missed him, and that it pained her greatly, but it pained me even more to see her cry.

Visitation with our father was every other Saturday, and I really wish I could say that I was excited to go, but the thought of *her* made my stomach turn. He lived only two towns over, so the drive was short. The outside of the house seemed nice enough, but it wasn't what was on the outside that mattered at all. Our first stop was his garage. He walked us up a little stone walkway, and I glanced over at the huge yard. Without me even saying a word my father looked over at us and said "Now, we can't be playing in the yard because the dogs shit all over the place and we don't want you tracking it all over the house." My first thought was *well, that really sucks*, but then I realized that it was more of a warning than anything else.

When we walked in there was a huge 1969 Chevy Camaro 728 that he had been restoring. It was a great hobby of his, and boy was he proud to show it off. He was painting it a sparkly red finish so that its beauty was most defined. As he yammered on about the glory of his car my eyes were wandering the room. He had old posters of Yvonne De Carlo, a.k.a. Lily Munster from the 1964 hit television sitcom "The Munsters". He loved her look. She had always been kind of oddly beautiful to me, too. He had hung pictures of all the cars he had restored to show off his work, but to who was my question. He used to have a friend named John Alonzo back in the day. They would restore cars and sell them for extra cash, but I hadn't seen John since he moved to that house. I knew my father always wanted the best cars for himself; he would use the profit to go and get himself new cars.

As we walked out of the garage and to the house I didn't even look at his yard. It was too much of a waste to me. If he never intended it for us to play on, then why bother?

As we walked into his house, my jaw damn near dropped in horror. I had always wondered where he was and what he had been doing in the months since he went MIA, and now I knew. It was the most horrific thing I had ever seen! Utterly speechless, we proceeded inside of the house.

You can't even make something like this up; they had seventy-eight cats, four dogs, six birds, and a tiny chipmunk. I truly could not believe my eyes. There were animals crawling on the walls of that house, and I thought I was going to be sick. Even worse than the animals was the scowling woman standing in the doorway. She was so unwelcoming that she made me trip over my feet as she hurried us in and warned us about leaving the door open because of the cats. I looked behind me to check, but I really wanted to run out of the door instead of closing it. We got a very short tour of the house, which was pretty much just rooms filled to the brim with cats. Sick ones, stray ones, feral ones; they all had a story and a place to live. Her sick mother lived in the back of the house, and there was no proper introduction. We had been directed by my father to sit on two stools in the kitchen, because all of their chairs were being occupied by cats. A bit confused, I sat down. I just sat there, watching in horror. Speechless, my eyes watched her. Pauletta opened a cabinet and I was hoping that she was going to have snacks for us, but boy, again I was baffled. In the cabinet where the snacks should have been were rows and rows of canned cat food. Orange, blue, pink, yellow- I never knew there were so many options! They had them all. On the counter in front of me there were rows of dishes holding hard cat food in any flavor that they wanted to choose. I went to pet a couple of the cats, because I actually did like animals; just not this many. She used a cracked, shaky tone with me and told me to leave them alone. Now I was getting angry. That was just wrong! How dare her. It was like a petting zoo, and I couldn't even touch? Since I had nothing else to do, I stared and started to analyze her. She was the ugliest creature I had ever seen in my life. I never wanted to be mean, but she was mean to me, so I already knew that liking her was out of my hands. As she sifted through the colorful array of cans, I noticed that at the very top of her short, frail, orange-reddish, faded out hair was a balding spot. It looked as though she had dyed it one too many times. Short and round was her figure, and there was nothing feminine about that way that she stood at all. It was awkward and plump. She has two kids of her own, (boys), so I didn't expect her to be slim, but gosh they were late teenagers by now! I met them in passing a few times. One was older with dark hair and glasses- Tommy. The other, Mitch, was thin and had the same shortness as his mother. Their father had died a few years back in some freak accident before she met my father, which explained why she already had a house. Well, I guess when he died she spent all of her time becoming a depressed cat hoarder. The widow card was what she had played with my father, and it all made sense now. She had money, the one thing that my father loved most in the world.

My father stood in front of me, holding two kinds of Chef Boyardee and since I knew that there were onions in the raviolis I opted for the beeferoni. I hated onions and everyone knew it, but no one ever fully accepted it, since they liked them. Onions turned my stomach and instantaneously made me want to puke. I would always get a whirl of nausea and my mouth would swell up with sickness. I didn't like it one bit. Mushrooms were also on my list. They reminded me of slippery slugs that you had to choke down your throat, so I would have the same reaction. I hated two of the worlds most commonly used ingredients.

They were loved by almost everyone in the America and put in just about everything, so pretty much I was screwed from the get go on that one. My mother knew how I felt, but she never really knew how to honor my requests. I'm pretty sure that she would have lied, stolen and cheated to get her way. Giving her arm may have even been an option at one point. I would go on strike and refuse her food and because I was so thin she would give in and give me Campbell's Chicken Noodle Soup and salads for years. I would eat hamburgers and things like that, as long as they had no onions, but other than that I stood my ground. My father knew that I would choose the beeferoni because it was safe, so my brother, who loved onions, gladly took the ravioli. He directed us to the living room and sat us on the floor. I was hoping we could sit in chairs and talk to him like we used to, but he had other ideas.

I was actually enjoying my bowl of saucy macaroni when across his big screen, which I knew that he was proud of, (he was boasting again), teenagers began getting murdered in their dreams! He had razor sharp knives as hands and his face was burned right off and had become a raw pink skin tone. He was scary! Freddy Krueger was the most awful, evil demon that a mind could think up and it was a terrifying experience. I went into the bathroom, choked up on my own terror, and cried.

There were really no words for that day, the things I saw or the things that had happened, and of course later on my mom wanted to play twenty questions. I told her about the cats and what we ate and the car he was fixing up, but never about the horrible movie. I really couldn't decide what was worse; the fact that my father had left my mother for a horrid cat lady, or if I would even be able to close my eyes tonight in fear that Freddy was coming to taunt, maim and murder me in my sleep.

Christmas Eve

Spending the next few months watching my parent's behavior was hard. They were so childish, and they fought over every little thing with my brother and I caught in the middle. With Theo being gone, my mom was an easier target for conflict, and there was no longer a middleman to do the every-other-Saturday transfers. Often my father would bring Pauletta to make my mother angry, and it worked. It drove her crazy every time, and he knew it. My parents didn't care about my brother or me. They hardly ever asked how we were. My brother was at the age where he was becoming a major nuisance, and everyone was annoyed. Erick made it unbearable to even be in the same room as him. He would lie if he was bad and break things and when I told, he would punch me in the arm. I really wanted nothing to do with him and neither did any of the family. I could really see Victor's patience beginning to blow short with him, because he started getting a firm tone. When we were stationed in our regular spots on the floor eating our Chef's and watching classic American horror films, Erick would try to get up and Vic would quickly slam him back without question. So he was left next to me to be a pest, but in a way I was glad that he had to watch the horror too. They did have a big, fake Christmas tree in their living room that sparkled and dazzled with strings of blinking lights, which made me sad because we had no tree at our house. I felt let down; I really liked theirs.

Pauletta had baked a birthday cake, but it wasn't mine, it was her youngest sons. We shared the same birthday. It was a lemon-lemon cake with red writing that said "Happy Birthday Mitch!" and in the very bottom corner "and Jaycee", which was how I knew it wasn't mine. How could he?

Even though the cake was his, it still tasted really good, and I thanked her. Man, even on Christmas Eve she was so on edge. I really couldn't figure her out. She had a good man, a house, a million cats and kids that came over, but she was still so nervous and unwilling to smile. It made me uneasy.

They did get me a present. It was a doll that had a crank on the back that made her hair grow when you turned it, but I was so disappointed because it wasn't the actual doll that was on T.V., but some dollar store junk that probably cost less than the ice-cream that had gone with the cake. I wanted to cry when they asked me how I liker her, but I swallowed it and said that I loved her. Being ungrateful wasn't going to make anyone happy, especially on Christmas Eve. In the car on the way home I asked my mom if we could put up the tree that we had boxed in the basement, but she said "Jaycee, I haven't really had time this year and you know that. Theo's gone, and it's just not a good year to." I looked down at the doll that my mother had already called junk and I felt bad for her. It wasn't her fault that whoever had made her took no love and care with her. She didn't deserve to be a misfit. I gave her already knotted hair a brush out of her face, and it almost looked as if she smiled.

Later that night when everyone was asleep, dolly and I snuck down to the basement and dragged the large, rectangular box up the stairs, and then went back down and dug out the Christmas ornaments. It took me forever, but I found them buried under boxes of boxes. I also found a card that made me chuckle. It had Santa on the front and inside it read, "Money's short, times are hard, here's your fucking Christmas card." *That's for damn sure* I thought. Before I went to bed that night there was one more trip to the basement, and that was for the giant Santa Clause that should have been placed in our yard. It even lit up, so I plugged it in and leaned it against that couch thinking, *now it's Christmas.*

When my mother and brother woke up they looked at the tree, smiling, and my mother said, "Did you do this Jay?" I bashfully nodded my head, and then we all laughed because I had put all of the branches on facing the wrong way, so the tree looked limp all the way around. They fixed them and said, "There!" and each hugged and thanked me. Mom even apologized for not making the time; that was all I really wanted. That and breakfast.

With a new year upon us, I heard everyone talking about resolutions and plans for change, so I made a resolution of my own. From now on, when my parents would want to talk bad to us about each other I would stop them. Putting my foot down was all that I had left. They were trying to torture each other through kids, and enough was enough! When they started in I would change the subject or walk away. Mean doesn't even describe how bad they would make each other sound, but I knew the truth. They were both bad in different ways.

The visits to my father's house became quite repetitive. They involved the same things over and over; beeferoni, a hag who would stare at us scowling, psycho horror, and us over and over and over. I wasn't sure how much longer I could go on without putting an end to it. Seeing the look on my fathers face was hard. He didn't really want us; we were becoming a chore and a burden. Now that so much time had passed and my mom knew I wasn't talking about things, there wasn't much to battle over anymore. Pauletta was the worst to be around. She smelled putrid, and her rotting teeth were making me sick. She always wore a gross nightgown, and no bra, ever! I really wanted her to tie up those flapjacks. Her toes stuck out of dirty, pink old lady slippers, and I could see the rot on her toenails. All this beast of a woman cared about was her damn cats, and it showed. Cats, cats, cats. So many cats that it was like an epidemic over at that house. They would just keep crawling the walls! My mother started to see that I was becoming unhappy and I don't know how she did it, but our visits slowed with him. I could tell that this pleased her, because she knew that I was starting to see who my father really was.

Spring, 1990

Now that we barely saw Victor my mother was in a bit of a jam, because she still had to work on the weekends. She spread out the time between sitters and grandparents, but we still missed her. One day we were playing in our backyard and our neighbor- the one I had met at the wedding- walked over and started talking to us. He asked about Theo and how long he was gone and of course my mother knew the exact date of his return. I heard her say "soon" and a sigh of relief left her. He asked my mom if he could come over sometime and play cards with her, and she said, "That would be a great idea!" because she was lonely. Thinking that he was kind of old for my mom, I continued to play in our turtle sandbox until there was a pair of black, shiny shoes standing near me. Looking down he said, "Hello Jaycee" and nodded. I went back to playing. He was kind of a stranger to me, and I never liked strangers. He walked away into his yard, and I wondered why he never said hi to my brother, who was sitting beside me, smashing my sand castle.

The phone began to ring more, and that meant that the time was nearing for Theo's homecoming. I overheard her telling him that she had invited our neighbor over for cards later. He never minded, because what was my mother going to do with a seventy-three year old? So, with no threat in mind, he agreed that it would be fun for her. Hearing him lifted her up. The neighbor came for cards time and time again, staying longer and longer, getting to know her. Before every game he would come over to where my brother and I were sitting, say hi, and try to make small talk, but we really paid him no mind because television was much more important. One night that he came he invited me over to the table and I was surprised. *Why me?* I wondered. I couldn't even play cards. Jokingly, he handed me the deck and told me to shuffle it, but of course I couldn't, so he showed me how. Slowly he shuffled the deck, then faster and faster until he had dealt out their game. "Next time you'll get better" he said, and off to bed I went, thinking that maybe if I practiced shuffling enough, I'd get it. They played about three times a week, so seeing him was becoming more frequent. They played blackjack, and sometimes spades and cribbage. I liked looking at the red and green pieces on the board, and Len would let me sit on his lap and move all of the pieces up and down the thin, rectangular board. I pretended that they were me, jumping over my classmates in leapfrog. I loved leapfrog so much! Then my mom would dismiss me. Theo came home and they would all play cards together. It looked like they were really having fun. My mom had never been so happy! She was chomping at the bit to get to the bar with her long awaited new husband like old times, though. The only problem was that we really had no late-night sitter. Lucky for her, Len had offered his services when he heard her dilemma. We were already bathed and in out PJ's before we saw him walk through the front door. He used a special knock- da dun, da, dun, dun, dun, dun- so from now on, we would know it was him. We practiced shuffling while he let Erick happily melt his brain in front of the television set, and when I was done playing I would join my brother, because I always knew that he was letting us stay up later than we should.

Len started watching us once a week so that my parents could go out. Erick really started acting out. He was so fresh, and Theo was not handling it well at all. He got the belt when he hit me or disrespected my mother. It was so scary to watch Erick fight Theo until Theo finally won. I never wanted that belt either, but somehow my mouth would always spout off something he didn't like and I would get it too. It hurt, and I would fight him off, but he was strong. It made me hate Theo.

He was the one who needed the belt, not me. He swore like a sailor, and he drank and smoked. I did none of those things. Erick was always hitting me, and in return he would get hit, and they both made me cry. Looking at them hurt. I'm not sure why my mother let this happen, but she really let me down. The more beatings that happened the more damage was being done, and I blamed her. She was supposed to protect her children, not defend the attacker. I couldn't understand. I asked to go to my grandmother's as much as I could, but there was a catch…

You see, my grandmother's house was great. Actually, it was amazing! We swam and went shopping and ate the best food; she was a great cook! I loved sitting at her kitchen table, watching her. Everything that she did was careful. If she spilled, she wiped. If it went on the floor, it was picked up right away. There was always a system, so smooth and clean. Country music always played while she cooked in that perfect kitchen. It was ok, but sometimes I wished she would put on some pop, just to switch it up. When she got all of the hot, delicious food put out just the way she wanted it, she would have me go and retrieve my grandfather, which was never an easy feat. Grandpa, just like grandma, liked doing things on his own terms, not hers, and this caused friction. He would come into the house, walk right past the hot food, raise and eyebrow at me, and go wash up. Grandma and I always got started before him because if we waited we would starve. Halfway through our meal he would walk through the kitchen door, grab the newspaper off of the top of the microwave oven, sit down, and open it to read as his food got colder and colder. My grandmother's patience grew short, and I could see why; he was so rude! We talked to each other, and every now and again he would put the paper down and say a few words or laugh or smile. Sometimes he would push her and she would mention divorce or say that maybe if she were gone he would be better off. It pained me to see her break down, but I knew that people had their limits. One thing that she did that drove me nuts, though, was mocking him behind his back and look to me for a response. It wasn't fair to put that on me, and I didn't really know how to react, so I would just smirk or huff in agreement.

She would do the hand flapping and the lip movements whenever they disagreed, but I always thought there must be another way.

We would always go to Catholic Church on Saturday nights, and sitting there with my Grandparents made me feel both happy and really bored. The Priest spoke about how Jesus Christ the Lord is connected to everything, but I never really understood the hour-long sermon. It was simply too long. When we were done we always drove to a place called Ice Cream Lane, where there was a big red barn with a gazebo in the front, and it was beautiful. Inside my nostrils would fill with the delicious scent of fresh, homemade ice cream. My favorite was pink peppermint stick. My grandma always had two big scoops of butter pecan, and grandpa would have a scoop of chocolate. It was called Milo's Dairy, a small town hidden treasure, and it was a child's delight! That night, no matter how hard I had tried to avoid it, nightfall was upon us. This was the catch to staying at grandma's house. I hated night! My grandmother had her nightly routine, and so did grandpa. He was in bed by seven-thirty every night, and grandma and I would watch "Murder She Wrote" and "Colombo" until about nine o'clock, and then it was time. She would start getting the blankets out, and I knew that no matter how much I begged there was no changing her mind. Over the years begging had just gotten old, and so had I, which was her reason for making me stay in the room her daughters had once shared. "Please Grandma, shut the windows!" The answer was always the same. "No! It's too hot, and you need the fresh air!" As she left she would always try to close the door and I would freak out and say "No! Leave it open!" A crack was the best she would do, and it was never enough. I would lie there, holding myself as tight as I could with the blankets pulled as high over my head as they possibly go, almost to the point of no air. If I needed to pull them down it would only make it worse I would look at the three low-to-the-ground windows and imagine the worst! The fear was so overwhelming at times that I would sweat under the covers, terrified and shaking. Praying to God became my only hope. We would talk for hours, and I would just beg for the night to end.

"Our Father who art in heaven, hallowed be thy name. Thy kingdom come, thy will be done, on earth, as it is in heaven. Give us this day our daily bread, and forgive us our trespasses, as we forgive those who trespass against us. And lead us not into temptation, but deliver us from evil. God bless Grandma, Grandpa and me, Mom and Dad and Erick, and everybody in the whole entire world. Lord please, please, please make sure that we are all safe, healthy and protected and let us be together always. Amen and thank you, thank you, thank you and thank you again."

When I woke up in the morning I would sigh a huge breath of relief and run to the kitchen where grandma would already have a bowl of fruit loops and OJ waiting. She would say "How did you sleep?" and I would say "Ok, but could have been better if we were together." But before she even gave me a chance to state my case, she would kindly remind me of my age; eight. I would look up at the ceiling, and he always knew that I was thankful for another day.

Usually I would last about a week before asking to go home in the summer. Spending six sleepless nights was about all I could take. Knowing my Gram always wanted more from me made it hard, though. If only she knew my terror.

By the time we got to my house my mother was happy and wanting to see me, but to see her mother? Not so much, because the questions were about to get asked. Did she have enough money? Did she need food, or clothes, or lunch? My Mother almost always accepted one of her offers. Into the car we piled, and my brother was just waiting to annoy me in the back seat. Erick drove my grandmother, and she never hid it either. She had no problem telling him that if he was going to misbehave that he would get nothing and that I would get everything, which is what happened in almost every case. It did make me feel a bit sorry for him until I understood that being a jerk truly got him nowhere with anyone in our family. Erick did favor my grandfather, because grandpa let him act like a boy without care. I was always grateful for that, because I wanted the best for him. He wouldn't have to be that way if he was taught differently. It's not like Victor or Theo were any good for him. Even my neighbor Len couldn't be bothered with Erick. He would always invite me in and not him, and I knew why. Or, at least I thought I did. Erick never showed that he cared, because he loved to play outside. It was really the only time that he could burn off some of his energy without getting yelled at or beat by Theo for it. For the most part we were free to roam the front and the back yard. As long as we promised to stay close, it was fine. Mom knew we were safe enough… but did she really?

Eight. Being eight was really such a fun age. I loved school and care bears. My Little Ponies were my favorite play-toys because they had the most colorful hair, and just looking at them made me happy. Playing outside was really where my heart was. We didn't have very many kids in our neighborhood, so I had to play alone. Wishing for friends had always been a dream. A little girl like myself would have been perfect. There was a boy who had moved into the very front house with his single mother. His name was Billy, and he had a stutter. We played when we saw each other, but he really had a hard time talking to me. I felt sorry for him because he was so nice to me. His mother was a less pleasant woman. She was strict with him. I could hear it in her voice when she called him in from play-time. He lived on a top floor, but I could still hear him say "Sssssooooorrrrrrrrryyyyyy Mmmmmooooommmmmm!" before she gave a strong whack. She would say, "I told you five-fifteen and now it's five-thirty!" But she knew we were there, and she knew that we had no wristwatches. She had a huge, black boyfriend and I wasn't sure he was the nicest guy either. I only saw him go in and out, but I could hear him yell and beat my friend too. It made me shiver to hear him in such trouble, and for no good reason. Poor Bill.

One day when I was playing up front, Len stuck his head out the front door and said, "Hey, can you come inside?" I looked around, over my shoulders, almost as if I knew that I wasn't supposed to, but he said "It's ok, I'll tell your mom on the phone that you're here" so in the house

I went. I examined his house. It looked and smelled old fashioned, like my grandmothers, but not nearly as nice or homey. I asked where his wife Lilly was, and he said that she was upstairs sleeping because she was ill. My reply was that Lilly was my middle name, and he said he knew, and that "that made me a very special little girl." But the truth is that I hated my middle name Lilly. I thought it was too old fashioned, and that flower was my all-time least favorite. When Len gave me the tour of his house he did let me see his wife. Her room was across the hall from his, just like my grandparents. Lilly asked me what I was doing there, and I said that he had invited me in. She said, "Ok, Jaycee can go home to her house now!" in a stern voice. I could tell that I was being a bother, and I didn't like it one bit. He showed me his bedroom next, and I noticed that his bedroom window had a straight-across view of my bedroom. I asked him if he could see me, and he said "Sure, sometimes, if you stand in view." That made me a bit uneasy, as it would make anyone whose neighbor had a direct view of their personal space. He had a huge wad of cash on his dresser, and he knew I was looking at it. I had never seen such cash, unless I went into the bank with my grandmother. We went back downstairs, and I asked to leave, mostly to respect Lilly's wishes. He insisted that I stay, but I really wanted to leave, so I did. Later that night my mother told me that she had spoken to Len and that it was perfectly okay to go in if I wanted to, but I knew otherwise. Lilly didn't like me there, but he never mentioned that to my mom, and neither did I.

When it was time for bed that night I shut my pink curtains extra tight, peekeing out the side, and saw a shadowy figure standing across the way.

The next day when I was playing on the side of the house, Len once again stuck his head out and invited me in. This time I was so bored that I agreed and in we went. Right away I said, "Are you sure Lilly won't mind?" He said that she was sleeping and that as long as I was quiet, she wouldn't mind. He let me explore the fridge and I found what looked like vanilla, chocolate and strawberry milk shakes, so I asked for one. He said they were Lilly's and that when she was sick this was all she could eat, but that I could have just one. Vanilla Ensure was my choice, but it had a chalk-like taste after one sip, so I decided that next time I would choose chocolate.

He let me watch television because I was getting bored, so I lay on my stomach with my hands on my cheeks and waited for a show of my liking to come on. He found Loony Tunes, and the silence began. About ten minutes into the cartoons, Len asked me to come over to where he was sitting in a brown recliner chair, so I popped up and went to his side. He asked if I wanted to play a game, so I asked what kind and he replied, "Show and tell!" I immediately said yes, because in kindergarten we did show and tell and it was my favorite game. We would bring things from home to share, and everyone had toys! His next sentence was much more serious, though. "Now, when we play this game, you cannot tell your mother, ever! She will hate you and me, and we will both get into so much trouble. Now, you wouldn't want your mom to hate you, would you?" My eyes quickly filled with tears. "No, no, I won't tell, I promise!" That was the most serious, solid promise that I had ever made, and it scared me! He said, "Now that we have rules, we can play. You lift up your shirt so I can see your chest." Confused, I did, and he was staring and staring. Then he said "Ok. That was the show part. Now remember, you can't tell or your mother will never, ever speak to you again." Nodding in agreement I was ready to go. When I got home my mother was in the kitchen smoking a cigarette. She asked how my visit at Len's was, and I said it was fine, never breaking my promise.

Age Nine and Beyond

As the year passed by, things really didn't make a whole lot of sense anymore. I thought that I always knew what the right and wrong thing to do was, but the truth is that I really had no clue. It was becoming a jumble in my brain. We saw our father maybe once a month on Saturdays. He stuck to the usual American Horror films and beeferoni. When he played the films I just let my mind wander to escape the blood and gore before me. I wished for some other kind of food; even a sandwich would have been nice, for Pete's sake! Pauletta was becoming uglier than ever. In my eyes all she cared about were those damn cats and at times I really wondered if she even loved my father at all. On top of that, my father would still bash my mother by telling me all of these awful stories about drug use and late nights and such to glorify him into being father of the year. But he never knew that I never once bought it because I knew him too well. Erick would lie over everything, just like him, and it really bothered me. Why lie? Telling the truth was the right thing, wasn't it? But then I would think, "Who am I to talk? I've been lying too."

My parents still played cards with Len at least once a week, and I could tell that he was drawing closer to them each time, building trust. They had no idea why, but I did. He wanted me and me alone. When he came through the doorway he had a look in his eyes, and I knew what it was. He would grab me when my parents weren't looking, and it made me jump, so when I could get away I went straight to my room.

When I spent time in there alone I would melt crayons on my radiator and watch the colors drip. The hot wax would coat my fingertips, and they became my crayons. My mother would get angry when she saw the rainbow radiator, but she knew that she couldn't stop me so she never argued with me unless the wax hit the floor. But even then she could scrape it off. I always wondered if she knew that was a sign. Then I thought that maybe if I gave her an explanation that she could help me, but the fear burned in the back of my mind that she would hate me.

He was getting more adventurous with my body. With my pants around my ankles, he would take his index finger and scrape it around the insides of my small, female body part. When I had enough I would ask to be released and he would agree, then give me a few dollar bills as a reward. The dollars were good for me because I could go to the small universe market, a small store through a pathway between Len's house and mine. The little market had so much to offer; candy cigarettes, fireballs, bazooka comic bubblegum, and my favorite, the huge kosher dill pickles that they had in the deli case. Seventy-five cents was all that they were, and I had plenty to cover the cost. Usually if Erick was willing to keep his mouth shut and not ask how I got the money, we would split the goods, except the pickle. He didn't dare ask. We were so hungry that the newfound cash helped ease the pain of what was happening to me.

As the year passed on, he would try to get me into his house as much as he possibly could without being caught by my parents. That was usually about two or three times a week, and he would touch, feel and scrape my body. If I didn't show, he would find me. He always found me. His face became known in and around my house and I had a very uneasy feeling when he was around me. When I saw him come through my doorway my heart would jump out of my chest, because he was my hunter. Sometimes I would even picture him in a hunting safari suit with a shotgun. He was beyond alarming. On the weekends I would beg my mother to go to grandmas because as much as I hated sleeping in that terrifying, dark spare room with open windows, getting away was well worth it. Time never really mattered anymore because it never seemed to end, but just get worse. Hate and walls of anger were growing inside of my heart and the pain just got stronger. My room was the safest and most quiet place for me. My heart and head could rest there, away from it all. Mostly my room was messy. Cleaning it was such a big job. I always wished that my fairy godmother would come and wave her magic wand just like she did for Cinderella so that everything in my life would be perfect. Believing in her couldn't hurt, I thought.

When I did get it clean going outside was my reward. Fresh air was good! I would play on the opposite side so that he couldn't find me. We had a rock wall, so playing the risk game was the most fun! The rocks weren't exactly in a wall formation or the same height. They were all different shapes and sizes. Some were sharp and jagged, but I never cared because it thrilled me.

My legs looked terrible and this made me sad because it was partly my fault and partly Theo's. We had a couple of indoor and outdoor pets. One was a big orange and white striped cat named Chester who knew how to pee in the toilet, partly because my parents were so bad about changing his litter box. I would get so frustrated with the odor and mess of that thing that they kept in the back hallway. It was so smelly that it was like a punch in the face when you would walk by. When I would ask mom to scoop it she would say that Theo was going to do it later, but he never did. We also had a dog that Theo surprised us with. He had him wrapped up in his coat when he picked us up from school one day. We loved him. His name had already been picked out by Theo, who had named him Oreo, and we liked it. He was a cocker spaniel that looked like an Oreo cookie, and he had so much curly hair. His one flaw was that he had kind of droopy eyes, and you could see the red part. I felt sorry about his flaw, because he was so cute. Now, the problem was not our pets but our parents. They were so lazy when it came to the maintenance parts, like taking the dog out, and so was Erick! Oreo. was a puppy and the responsibility was too much for me alone, so I would tie him out all day because all he would do was piss all over the floor and I really couldn't take it anymore! When I was younger we had had a lab, Raisins, who would poop all over the house, so eventually we had to say goodbye to him. I was getting a sense of familiarity with Oreo. Maybe if he had the proper training from the get-go, he wouldn't be so bad.

Fleas. So many tiny, itchy fleas. They had become an infestation in our house! They bit me the most, and when I told my mom and Theo that I was being eaten alive he said that it was all in my head, just like the onions. He never believed me. He always thought that I was lying just to cause trouble. My heart sank. Couldn't he see the bloody bites up and down my body? Itchy fleas were the worst things that ever happened. They would bite my skin and drive me crazy! The only way that my parents were going to believe me was if I showed them. A glass jar would do the trick, I thought. I could fill it with fleas and show them. Then they couldn't argue. I never thought that the animals wouldn't agree with this idea. They fought me. Holding them down wasn't easy, but it had to be done. It was easy to see the fleas. Black and red, they stuck out mainly from the cat's forehead. I looked at the fleas and studied their mean bodies. They were so gross, yet staring at my enemy before I tried to crush it to death was a great satisfaction for me. They didn't go down without a fight, though. The cat and flea despised my efforts, so filling the jar was unsuccessful, ineffective, and a pointless waste of all of our time. The best I could do was find the biggest one and pinch it in between my fingers, then run and show my mother before it could jump away. She would yell at me to go and flush it down the toilet right away, so my next attempt was to show Theo the underbelly of the cats. They had black eggs that looked like dirty spots all over their furry bodies. The only thing that he did was yell at me and tell me how wrong I was! Day in and day out about the fleas it was "it's all in your head, and you're making it out to be more than what it is", again and again like a stupid broken record. It was then that I realized that my stepfather was the most ignorant bastard that had ever walked into my life.

Chinese food was my favorite, and he knew it. He knew that my hunger could be awardable with the touch of my body, and he was right. We could never afford to eat take out like that, but every now and then my mother would spend the money. She ordered shrimp chow mien with no onion, mushrooms or scallions, and no onions in my rice. It was my favorite! He knew how I liked it because I stressed that onions were the enemy. He let me decide if the award would happen before or after he picked up the delicious dish of hot take out. After was my choice, because I was too hungry to stand there while he rummaged through my parts. When the food would arrive he let me have the brown paper bag to myself, drowning the celery and shrimp with soy sauce. My mouth would salivate because it looked so delicious. He put the television on and I ate and ate until my belly said enough. There was always some left to finish, but I just couldn't. I never brought the leftovers home because the fear and guilt of my hungry brother being jealous made me feel too bad. So into the garbage it went. After taking as much time as possible, it was time. After all, that was the reason that I was there. He would try to look me in the eye to see if there was some kind of true pleasure from me, but there was nothing. It was awful, and never once did his rough fingers feel good inside of me. He asked if I liked it and I just shrugged my shoulders and shook my head, but his touch was sickening to my over-full stomach. When he pushed around on my insides the overwhelming urge to puke was not far from the back of my throat, so I had to make him stop. It was intense, and my limit was reached. He became angry with me, saying, "Fine, that one was a freebee and the debt was paid off, but just this time!" Later that night in my room I thought, "Why should I owe him? He touched me!" My anger was growing because my stomach still felt sick, and not from the food, but from him.

One person who never let me down was my Grandma. She would take me away, and not just to her home in Newport, but to another home, far away. Well, ok, not exactly far away, but more like an hour and some minutes, in Sandwich Massachusetts. Her mother, my great-grandmother, lived there. We drove the long drive every other week to see her and I never minded one bit. My grandma La Roo was a one-hundred-percent Polish woman, born and raised catholic. She was very much into the lord. She even had holy water to bless yourself with when entering into her home. Gram was in her late eighty's and still lived alone in the home she once raised her daughter in. Above her lived my mother's oldest sister, her husband, and their baby, so Gram had plenty of help. Plus, my grandmother would take her to the store on our visits, so she had everything. Her house really felt like a great-grandmothers house should. She knitted, and she had a candy dish and cookies. What I loved most was the smell of Polish cooking filling her home. Gram always had meat and cabbage pierogi's, stuffed with butter and onions. (Hold my onions, of course.) We never left hungry. The food was from the heart, and Grandma Roo made sure of it! Gram always sat me down and explained how important it is to believe in the Lord and prayer. Her teachings were wise and she knew the way, so I always listened. Knowing as much information as she did really had meaning to me, because I could only hope to be that wise one day, and maybe teach my great-grandchildren, just as she did. Knowing that God was always going to be there wasn't a bad thing. In fact, knowing that I wasn't alone was a blessing.

There was a mixed race of people in Sandwich, but mostly Puerto Ricans and blacks. Some seemed to be very rough around the edges, but that never once swayed my great-grandmothers decision to stay in her area. She figured that shouldn't affect her. She had her rights and her mind was made up, even though I always knew that there was a growing danger around her place. There was a little Puerto Rican boy named Jose that lived next door and he liked when we came to visit very much because we could talk through the wire fence that kept the yards apart. He mostly always smiled at me, and sometimes my head thought that he wanted more. Liking that feeling of being wanted kept me going back to that fence every time that we visited my great-grandmother.

On the drive home my grandmother was always very quiet, probably because there was always something that her mother said about her life to offend her. So she would stew about it during the ride back, and it made me feel bad for her, because she really was trying her best at this crazy thing called life. I think that every mother wants to know that her mother is proud when her children are grown and they become a grandmother. They mostly spoke to each other in Polish, so it was hard to know the exact cause of their arguing. It did make me feel left out when they spoke in tongue, and whether they knew it or not, I was going to figure it out.

The summer was quickly approaching and I had completed my fourth grade year. This was the best time of year for me because I could be with my grandma, away from him, Theo, Erick and the fleas! Theo had actually caved in and bombed the house two times, so the fleas weren't as bad, but they were there and I was sure that when summer returned, so would they. But none of that mattered because my grandpa would have the beautiful, eight-foot in-ground pool open for me, and I would dive right in and wash away the dirty feeling that the fleas and Len left on my body. Swimming was my favorite thing about summer; it was my heart! They had the best pool in the world, and it was all mine. My grandma had a cement patio around it, so you could lounge, eat, read, relax and nap. I would do all of that at my Newport home. My favorite things to eat by the pool were the sandwiches that my grandmother made. She always used the best tomatoes, lettuce, turkey, provolone cheese, bread, and light mayo; too much would gross me out! She cut them perfectly and served them with chips and a pickle. My mom never made them that way. Like everything else she made for me, they were so good. I definitely appreciated her cooking, and she knew it by the empty dishes. One thing that my mother had never learned from her was how to cook. My mother's idea of cooking was just throwing things together, even if it made zero sense. The base of almost all of her soups and stews was ketchup. Good thing that I grew up liking ketchup, because almost everything that she served me got covered in the red, tomato goodness... and extra salt and pepper, of course. Mom never cooked for grandma, because she knew that there was nothing to compare. When mom, Theo and Erick came to visit and use the pool on really hot days in the summer, grandma would run with me and my mother to the local Kentucky Fried Chicken and spoil us with the juicy, crunchy, delicious fried goodness and sides to boot! She really did love my family. To do such a thing was a joyous occasion to me. After dinner, talk of me coming home was always an issue, and in some cases getting a good night sleep was what I wanted and needed. I really couldn't get any sleep in that room alone. Knowing that I could get a few nights of proper sleep, I would do it. This made her sad. You could see it in her beautiful eyes, and it broke my heart. We loved each other so much that being apart hurt us both.

He always knew of my return home, and that front door would get a knock no later than an hour after I got there. It would piss me off, because he was such an intruder on my time with my family. My mother spent time shooting the shit with him and not me, and it made me jealous as anything. He always convinced her that she needed a break and that a night out was in her best interest. "Screw that!" I thought. She just got me back- what a waste! It was easy to see that he had clouded her judgment. He was so good at pushing her around without exposing the truth about what he was really doing to her daughter. Part of me wished that she would see that truth, and the other part of me held so much fear of her hating her only daughter. I was at a loss. The only thing that I could do was hide from him at my grandmothers and in my room until he found me again. His wife died that summer, so he was very busy with that for at least two weeks. I went back to trying to live a normal life and started playing with the kids in my neighborhood more freely. It was nice to not be under his control. Trying to play with Erick was impossible, though. He would torture me, and he had the most annoying way about him. He always told lies, and not just to me, but to his teachers and friends. He told great big stories that were so fictional and beyond made up that not even your imagination would believe it. At first I thought that he did it to be cool, but apparently telling all of the neighborhood kids that he was half Puerto Rican didn't go over so well. He just looked like an idiot, and it was so embarrassing to be around him. Everyone always looked to me for the truth, and I always had it. He had a couple of friends that saw through his bullshit. They were kind of cute. They took no interest in me because I was younger, but they wanted to know.

The truth is, I don't think that Erick knew how to deal with the pain of our father or having Theo step in and put his hands on him. I think that he coped by making his life something that it wasn't, the complete opposite of what our reality was. After a while, I'm pretty sure that in his mind he started to believe all of the lies and stories that he made up. He would convince himself, and I truly felt sorry for him because he never had any guidance, or anyone to properly show him the way. With Theo you could never get a word in edgewise, so I always wondered who was going to help poor Erick. He was becoming seriously screwed up.

Fifth grade was the game changer. Things were much different now than they had been in the past. New things were happening, and realizing how to deal with them would be my biggest challenge yet. It all started in my fifth grade homeroom. Having the sweetest teacher that the fifth grade offered was a good start. Her name was Mrs. Beavers, and she was so sweet and pretty. Her hair was a short, brown, bob cut. She wore long, floral print dresses, but not the out dated kind like the teachers from my past had. She had a very caring way about her, and I was thankful for that. I was shy, but I always managed to make a few good friends, but I was never sure how, since my parents still couldn't afford super nice clothes or name-brand things for me. Still, somehow there were always kids in much worse shape than me, and I knew that their parents were far more broke than my parents had ever been. They were the ones who truly struggled, and I understood them more than they knew. I was always extra kind to them, never caring what the other kids thought. They would whisper mean things about their clothes and their hair and their shoes, and it bothered me. I knew for sure that they were hurting. In fifth grade, words became like knives and once the blade was in the real pain began. How did I know? Experience, of course.

Unfortunately, we had four periods together, and they were the most torturing periods of my life. Her name was Ariel Kibbler, and she always stressed that it was Arrrr-iel, not like Ariel from the famous Little Mermaid, which everyone loved whether they admitted it or not. I did! She was nothing like her anyway. The mermaid was kind and beautiful, and this girl was anything but. Her race was all she bragged about. Her skin was brown and her hair was black and had kink. I could overhear her all the time; everyone could. She talked about her dad being white and her mom being black. This was a huge advantage for the scowling, mean girl, because she could be friends with the outspoken blacks and Puerto Ricans of the school. She had an in, unlike a very poor white girl like myself. My first encounter with her was in the bathroom. She was fixing her hair, and I was just coming out to wash my hands. I could tell how she felt about me just by looking at her. By the look of disgust on her face, I knew that she thought that I was too ugly and unfit for her to be nice to me. When she walked out my heart hurt, because she was right. I looked in the mirror at my face and hair. I was awkward. My skin had started to develop blemishes that were becoming impossible to get rid of, and my hair was wavy, not curly and beautiful like the other girls. I would have killed for long, pin-straight hair. Red hair and freckles would have also been cute on me. I had a girl at my bus stop that had that look, and she was beautiful! Her name was Kelly, and she looked like a Kelly too. I felt so ugly compared to most of the girls in Ariel's group. They even had the best clothes and shoes. The one thing that I really envied about Ariel and her friends were their shoes. Man, shoes were the one thing that I loved most, and these were not just any shoes. They were Nike Air's, and they came in blue and white or black on black with white trim. They were so awesome looking. In big letters they said AIR on one side and MAX on the other. They were even cooler than the Fila shoes that were just as popular at the time in black and red. No, these shoes were the Scottie Pippen of shoes, one of the greatest wing defenders in league history. These things with the word AIR plastered across the side flew off of the shelves, but never once onto my feet. I just wanted to rip those shoes right off of her. She didn't deserve them. What made her so special that she could have the best shoes, friends and clothes? Well, nothing, and sooner or later I would get my own…hopefully.

Surprisingly, making friends was kind of easy. Kids liked my nice-girl personality, and it was a trait that even I couldn't deny. Having people to talk to was much easier than I had imagined. Kids wanted to joke and poke fun at each other, but not be mean about it. They just wanted to have fun, and it was nice. I really enjoyed the company of other normal kids my own age. It did make me wonder if Ariel was an asshole because maybe she was actually not normal. Maybe she had problems that nobody knew about that made her bitter. Just sitting in class with her made me uneasy, like she was picking me apart in her mind. What she never realized was that I picked her apart the same way; she was disgusting! Her laugh was horrid, and her nostrils flared like an angry dragon when an eruption came from her long, brown neck. It made me quiver in my desk, probably along with the rest of the fifth grade with the exception of her circle. They always laughed with her. And the fact that she would talk loud enough for the kids in the class to hear her conversations about them was really an embarrassment. It was intentional, and it was wrong. It was safe to say that I absolutely hated this bitch.

One thing that I wanted more than shoes was a toy. But not just any toy. This was the first animated, real-life toy that my eyes had ever seen, and I had to have it, no matter what the cost. JoJo, the walking, talking pup cost sixty dollars. There was no way in H-E-double-hockey-sticks that my parents could ever afford that type of toy. When I asked my Grandma, she even said that it was a ridiculous amount of money for practically nothing. This broke my heart. No one would ever understand how much I really needed this friend or how much it would mean to me to have something that would really be my own, forever. Before he used my body that day, I asked for a JoJo in a begging manner. I pleaded my case and he agreed, but at a high cost. I didn't like the sound of that, but I went up to his bedroom anyway, where he lay down on his bed and unbuckled his trousers. It was by far the most ugly thing that I had ever seen in my life. My stomach turned and the feeling of puking was racing up to my esophagus. He sat their touching it and making awful groaning noises until a yellowish explosion came pouring out, and I ran away. Flying out of that house I ran and ran and my heart pounded so loudly that my ears were screaming to stop. Without realizing it, I ran to the safest place that my legs could take me; the Secret Heart Church, which had a small park in the back. No one was there to see me throw up, and my heart was thankful for that. Since I was there I felt like now more than ever it was time to have a big talk with the Man upstairs.

The church was quiet and empty, but as I walked up to the half-naked man on the cross, he seemed to look at me. I had a strong feeling that he was looking down on me from where he hung, either way he knew I was there. Looking around at the dark red pews reminded me of the blood that Jesus had shed for us, and it made me feel thankful to him. Now, the thing was that I didn't really know all of the facts about my religion, so a bit of guilt had come over me. But I was trying my best, and that was all that I had to offer. Feeling confused and not really knowing what was happening to me made it hard to ask for an exact solution, but telling him the way that I felt about my terrible problem seemed logical. Telling him about my monster was something that I felt he knew. Pure evil and the devil were part of this mess. What I asked for was for it to stop, because hiding this and going through it alone with no one to tell was hurting me. "My Lord, please make the pain and suffering stop, and in return I will give you something, honesty." I knew that being honest with Jesus and myself was a step in the right direction.

He bought me the fucking JoJo dog, but it did not make me happy in the slightest. Looking at his face was hard, but what choice did I have, for fear of letting him see how much I hated his guts after what he made me watch him do to himself. He wanted to see me happy, but it was the opposite in my mind. Pretending to love the dog gave me a reason to ask to leave because, after all, she was a walking dog that needed to go out, so he agreed. I placed her on the ground and pushed the button on her leash and would you believe it? The damn thing kept falling over.

It didn't like the rock driveway, so I decided to take her home. Besides, I knew that he was watching… always watching.

When I walked through the door my mother said "Where the hell did you get that expensive toy?!" I panicked! "Chores, Ma. I did chores for Len, and he got me this!" As I showed her how it walked my mother still seemed unhappy with me, and that's what I feared the most. She explained that I should never, ever accept such extravagant gifts from anyone, and told me to go to my room. I could hear her slam the door, and I went to my window. She was having a firm talk with him, and I'm not sure what he said but she came home quick and she was calm now. She called me down and said that she was sorry and that she didn't realize how much hard work I was putting in over there. Stiff as a board she hugged me and told me to relax now, but all that I could do was ask to go back to my room. Sitting there and melting crayons on my hot radiator made the tears more colorful when they dropped from my eyes. After about four melted crayons the tears had all dried up, and it was time to play with my new toy. JoJo came with a brush, leash, and soft play bone. Now the thing that upset me was that on the commercial she was barking, but this dog said nothing. That was disappointing, because I wanted her to talk and she was not saying a thing. I decided to brush her, but that wasn't what I had expected either. The brush that they gave me kept getting stuck in her shaggy, long, white hair. The brush was so small that it was impossible to get through. Ok, so let see her walk. Well, she kept falling over after three steps. I really couldn't believe that JoJo was junk. It was pure trash and I was beyond pissed, so JoJo went for a flight across my room. What a bust! The T.V. lied and I would never fall for that shit again.

By the weekend I was beyond ready to leave my house and hit grandmas. My bags were packed by Thursday. Missing my grandma was the only real feeling that I had left. Going to see her kept me sane, because I was pretty sure that if he put his hands down my pants again I would go insane. Coloring was my outlet when boredom took over. Staying in the lines was an art to me; if I made one mistake, I would trash the whole page. For some reason it had to be perfect before it could even be looked at. Blending the colors was my favorite. It could make the pictures so much more than just regular. The basic colors were too plain. Pretending to put myself into the picture was another escape to me. Oh, how I wished to really be in a magical place. Grandma loved my pictures. She never hurried me to finish. She knew that I had to take my time, so she never offered for me to color on a day we were in a hurry.

When my grandparents fought, I really wanted to jump into my pictures. The fights usually ended with my grandmother in tears. She used to say, "If I drop dead then you will be really happy! I just wish I could die!" This hurt to hear her say, because I knew that she didn't mean it. How could she mean it? We all needed her more than she could ever know. My grandfather was a rude jerk to make her feel that way. If he could only put himself in her shoes then he would understand how much love she had to give. It also put me in the position to comfort, and it was hard for me because I hated to be in the middle. Telling her that there was no way that the world would be a better place without her was still not enough, because it should have come from him, not me! If only he was sensitive enough to understand that, then half of their problems could have been avoided. However there was one problem that would never seem to go away between them no matter what, and he was standing right in front of them, right in front of all of us.

Uncle Frankie, my mother's twin brother, rode up on his bicycle while I was playing outside on the stonewall. He had a tri-colored bandana on with some kind of dog on it. I remember trying to figure out if it was a bulldog or a mutt. He kind of startled me when he rode up; he kind of startled us all! He was nice to me and he called me Scooter, but I always felt bad because when he came around I was very guarded, so all he would get was a shy hello or a half-wave. When my grandfather discovered his arrival, the first words out of his mouth were, "Jesus Christ, what the hell do you want?" He never held back his dislike of my uncle's presence, and part of me could understand why. Frankie was greasy and dirty. He smelled of booze and body odor, and it made me really want to throw up my lunch! Grandpa would say "Get the hell out of here!" and Frankie would always reply, "Dad, I just want to say hi to Ma!" Just then my grandmother would fly out the front door and invite him in. With a look of disgust, grandpa would give an uneasy nod of approval. Great. Being left with grandpa when he was on edge made me feel just as uncomfortable as he was feeling. I knew that grandpa was mad by the way that he blew smoke out of his cigar; it looked like it was coming out of his ears! I grew bored, and I wanted to know why the heck he was here for a visit. When I walked in, grandma was hurrying around to make him as much food as she could before my grandfather came in; a sandwich, chips, cookies, a drink, anything that he wanted. As she struggled to get as much into his backpack as she could before being caught, they talked. Pretending not to listen or get caught myself, I kept my head down an acted busy. She asked many questions all at once, and he knew to answer them quickly.

"Where are you staying?"

"With a friend in Cranston."

"A girl or a guy?"

"A girl named Linda."

"Are you together?"

"She's my old lady, Ma, of course!"

"Are you guys clean?"

"Come on Ma, you know."

"Damn it, Franklin! I don't! Why the hell are you broke, then?"

"Ma, we got bills, and I'm trying to get a job."

"Well then why the hell do you smell like a damn booze hound?"

"Ma, I had like two beers before I came over, that's it!"

"You need to get a job Frank."

"Ma, I've been looking, but it's hard when you have no nice clothes or shoes."

That's when she would go and get her wallet from her pocketbook and rummage through for a fist full of twenties. His eyes lit up in an instant, and gratitude came spilling out like thank-you-vomit. She finished with, "Now go! Get the hell out of here!" At this point I felt pissed off, because even I knew that he was going to take the money and go have a party! My grandfather knew it too, and that's why he knew exactly when to walk in. Frankie also knew not to push his luck. Grandma always offered a ride for him to get back, but he always declined because he knew that he wasn't going right home. Leaving an awful stench behind, he was gone. This pleased me, but it wasn't over yet. Grandpa would ask how much and grandma would say only ten, sometimes fifteen, but even I wasn't stupid. Something I have never understood to this day was the fact that my grandparents had separate bank accounts. They were both equally secretive and greedy with their money, but only towards each other. They never wanted the other to know of their monetary affairs because it was sure to start a major fight. My grandmother explained to me that it was just to help her son because my grandfather had been giving my Aunt Dinah all of his money for anything that she wanted for years. This news made me mad, because it was clear that she was his favorite child, and for a parent to play favorites seemed wrong to me. My mother was always very cross with Aunt Dinah, and now I really knew why. It became a bit easier after that for me to understand that grandma wanted to be there for Frankie, so when he came around I wasn't as cold. He still gave me the creeps, though. After all, his status was being a drug addict and alcoholic. Now I had yet another family secret to keep, but put it in the back of my mind; I had enough of my own problems to deal with.

Things were changing on my body, and it was probably the most terrifying feeling that I had had yet. I was in the shower when I looked down and saw that my part was covered in thick, curly, black hair. It scared the crap out of me, and I wanted to know where it came from! It was ugly, and why the heck was it there? I had so many questions and not one answer. I couldn't ask my mother because, in my eyes, it was way too embarrassing. My cheeks were hot and red just at the thought of telling her this awful new information. My cheeks had started doing that a lot lately. My emotions were always so mixed now and Erick, Theo and my mother got the short end of my bad moods. You could say that I was somewhat of a beast. Part of the anger had nothing to do with my dysfunctional family; it was just me being moody. Chocolate and giant pickles from the universe market were all that I wanted, and Skore candy bars were my favorite. They were chocolate covered, crunchy toffee bars, and they were so good! Eating the chocolate off and sucking on the toffee made my day. Trying to figure out why I was craving these things was hard because I really had no clue. I did know one thing though; if I had hair down there, it must be other places, too. Sure enough, when I lifted up my arm there was no surprise in seeing a small amount of ugly, curly black hair there too, and the word just flew out; "Fuck!" Looking at my legs was all I needed to do to realize that I was growing up, and it seemed like it was happening very fast. The things that happened next were things that I could never have been prepared for; what girl could?

My skin was doing bizarre things too. The red dots were expanding on my face, and I couldn't help but touch them. It was almost like when I was five and I woke up with the chicken pox at my grandmother's house. There had been spots everywhere, but this time they were just on my face. It made me remember that my grandma had soaked my tiny, feverish body in an oatmeal bath. I decided to soak my face in my breakfast, but that only made me feel sticky and smell like maple syrup. It was then that I had to ask my mom for the expensive face wash that they sold at the supermarket, and she agreed. I also decided that something would have to be done about the smelly hair that was growing underneath my arms! When my mother went to the store, it was the perfect time for me to try this shaving thing out that I had seen her do on so many occasions as a little girl. I decided to do my arms first. I lifted them, trying to decide if it would be left or right first, but it didn't really matter since they were both getting done. It went well. Pressing the razor down seemed pretty easy, and it took the hair right off. There wasn't much there, of course, but it seemed easy enough that it gave me the confidence to shave my legs. I did my left leg first because I was right handed and that made the most sense to me. Flinging my leg up onto the toilet gave me the best balance. Now, there were two things that I should have realized before going any further. One was that the fresh razor that I had found while rummaging around under the sink was extremely sharp. The other was that I was trying to dry shave! Well, those two things that never crossed my mind really bit me in the ass! Blood, blood, blood. So much gushing, dark red blood. Panicking, I grabbed toilet tissue, but that was a bad idea because it was too fast and too much for the thin paper. A washcloth was close, so I grabbed that and pressed it to my shin where I had decided it made sense to start shaving. I looked under the soaking cloth and, holy shit, you could see the bone! I thought that I was going to faint. My mom was going to kill me! I thought that I was dead for sure. My mother burst through the bathroom door and said, "Jaycee what the hell is going on?" By her second question, a faint feeling washed over my body from the amount of blood I had lost, or the sight of it, or maybe both. After some extreme bandaging my mother called me to the kitchen and sat me down. I knew that this couldn't be good, and in my head played "Da-duh-DUM!", really loudly! She rummaged to the back of the cupboard and pulled out a package of store brand, hard chocolate chip cookies that not even Erick had known about. She poured two ice-cold glasses of whole milk, which took my mind off of the deep, throbbing cut in my shin. "Jay, it's time we had a talk." I'll never forget those words. It hit me; the cookies were to help soften the blow. Shit. She spoke about womanly changes, shaving, and the most God-awful thing of all; periods! Stuffing my face with cookies so I couldn't talk wasn't going to work for much longer because my belly was getting full, and quickly, because my nerves were eating too. Mostly she wanted reassurance that when the cursed event happened that I would make telling her a first priority, and I agreed. I limped to my room. The information that she had given me about this monthly period was going to be a lot to digest, and I needed to figure out what the hell to do with it.

When I got to my room I felt shaken by our conversation. I thought, *this is the most horrible thing. Why couldn't it happen to Erick?* He deserved it way more than I did! My room was an awful mess, so I decided that if I couldn't change the future, at least I could clean my room. Being a slob was not my thing. My parents were bad enough, so taking charge of my things was on me and only me. As I sifted through my clothes, her words still bothered me. She had said that my time of being a little girl was running out, but exactly how much time did I have left? With becoming a young woman, how much more responsibility would I have? It was not fair. My heart felt broken, but it was something that I was going to have to get over, and quick!

Sure enough, a week later I woke up on a Saturday afternoon and blood had stained my underpants. That scary feeling that I had in the pit of my stomach had turned into real pain now. There was a note left on the table from my mom.

Jay,
    You were sleeping so long, I didn't want to wake you up. You looked like you needed to rest. I'm down at The Sea Swirl having a quick drink, so if you or Erick need me, the number is 401-555-4620. Love,

                                    Mom.

Great! Now I had to call the bar. This was going to be a day. As I called the number, it was hard to turn the dial without being anxious. My parents still couldn't afford the new cordless phone that had come out the month before.

It was bizarre to call a bar for my mother when I needed her. A guy picked up and called her name. In the background I could hear a bunch of drunken sailors. When she spoke I was somewhat relieved, but kind of irritated at the same time. She asked if everything was ok, and I said, "No, Ma, I got my period. Can you come home?" What she did next was something that I could never forgive her for. She told the entire bar. My jaw dropped and I felt embarrassment wash over me as I heard her say

"Hey, guys! My baby's not a baby anymore! She got her period this morning! Awww! Jaycee, go under the sink and get the pads and don't freak out!"

I could hear the laughing and drunken comments. They weren't bad, but I didn't give a shit what those people had to say! My anger towards my mother grew after that. She truly had no regard for my feelings. She was a big, fat, blabbermouth, and I would never trust her with my secrets again.

When she came home she tried to coddle me like a baby, and it was so irritating. "Why did you tell the bar?" I asked. "It embarrassed me, and now I feel even worse, so thank you!" She replied with, "Oh Jay, stop it. They understood and had good advice!" I told her that it wasn't for her to share, and that they could keep their drunken advice and shove it. With the way that I stormed off she knew that she had broken my trust.

Now that my body was changing, my feelings began changing as well, especially towards him. I had to quickly make up excuses about why he couldn't touch me. Hiding had become a top priority for me; if I wasn't around then nothing bad could happen. School was okay, but my teachers quickly figured out that math was going to be a problem for me. What could be worse than that awkward moment when your teacher calls on you to do a simple problem, but you draw a blank and nothing comes out? Finally the others kids whispered me the answer because they couldn't stand the silence and wanted to move on. Every time this happened, sheer and utter shame washed over me from head to toe, my face turned beat red, and my heart began to race far faster than it should at my age. I wished I could disappear and die, but unfortunately that was not an option. It was clear that I was going to need extra help, and a lot of it. When the teacher sat me down the numbers started to jumble up and become one big, confusing mess in my mind. Even worse was the fact that the teacher was breaking it down to the fullest, but I was getting nothing. The tears began to flow; it was so frustrating to be in this situation, feeling like an idiot. The teacher would release me after that, and finally I could breathe again. I'm pretty sure that the sweat soaking my shirt was a sure sign that life was escaping me.

I was getting pretty tired of living in fear. If it wasn't math or the kids at school, it was Len. He asked so much of me and put a kind of pressure on me that felt so heavy. I could almost picture myself in the dessert heat, dragging through thick, golden sand with two tons of bricks on each side of my shoulders. It felt like some kind of punishment. He was over one night playing cards and my mother told me to go and take a shower. As I tried to avoid going near Len, he grabbed my arm and whispered in my ear that I needed to open my towel when I got out of the bathroom. I said no, and he squeezed tighter and said, "I need to see you fully naked!" I agreed just so that he would let go. I had chills from his lips being that close to my ear, and the smell of his tobacco breath made my stomach nauseous. As the hot water ran down my face, so did the tears. My life sucked, and I was in so far over my head. It seemed hopeless. I had no way out. Just then my mother knocked on the door and said "Jaycee, are you getting out? Len is leaving and wanted to say goodbye." Twisting the knobs to off, I took a very deep breath. I knew what I had to do, but I didn't want to. I came through the dining room and flew to the top of the stairs. There he was, in the doorway making the gesture for me to open my towel. I was scared of anyone else seeing, so he was only getting a second to peek. I stood there for a half a minute, counting with my towel open, watching in horror as he relieved himself right there in his pants. Running as fast as I could to the upstairs bathroom wasn't enough; it hit the floor everywhere. Everything that I had inside of me coming out still didn't take away the horrid images that were spread across his face when he did what he did in the door way; nothing could take that away. It was time to melt crayons. That always helped. It felt so good; the hot wax, the melted colors, the smell. That night was a 24-crayon kind of night, because sleep just wasn't an option.

As much as I hated math, school was a great escape for me. My friends help to take my mind off of the horrible things. Gym was kind of fun, because we all felt free and happy outside. We would all chat amongst ourselves about the days events and what we would be having for lunch. Lunch was my least favorite part of the day, though, because my mother packed me the worst lunches on earth. She mixed up this gross, awful deviled ham spread. I will never forget how the can looked; white with a tiny red devil on it. The white bread that she used was always stale, and I always gave the sandwich a swift toss into the trash.

The only other things in there were two celery sticks with peanut butter, two carrot sticks and sometimes an apple, which was not my favorite fruit, as well as applesauce, which I could have done without. Erick never seemed to mind the food. He ate everything. Jealous doesn't even describe how seeing the kids with hot lunch made me feel. Actually, it made me feel more starving than jealous. I asked Theo once if he could fill out the free or reduced lunch order form, but he said no, and that we would never qualify because we made too much money. The truth is, though, we were dirt poor and if he had tried I would bet my life that we would have gotten it with all of the bills that we had. We had our hot water shut off all the time, so how wouldn't we? The months of ice-cold showers were getting brutal, and it forced my mother to get a job waiting truck stop tables. The dollars were good, but she was never around and we still had barely any money. There were always bills. We did get to eat there now and again, though, and it was so good. There were french-fries galore, and Theo usually ordered us our favorite; cheeseburgers! The job was actually all right, until we needed a babysitter.

Before we left school one day, our teacher gave us a huge packet with a fundraiser inside. This was new to all of us. We turned through the pages of this wonderful catalogue, and there were so many glorious foods and candies that I could have licked the pages! Such splendor made all of our mouths water. Even better was the fact that the teacher announced that the more we sold the better prizes we could earn. The highest was a scooter, and it was so cool! This gave me something to keep me busy, which made me a very happy girl. I ran home that day, unable to wait to tell my mother. We could do it together! We could sell a lot of things and be rich with happiness. My mother was in bed because she had worked all night, so I quietly waited at the edge of her bed waiting for some movement, but there was nothing. She must have had a few beers before she went to bed, because she was out. Theo came in and told me to leave because she needed to sleep. I didn't argue for fear of getting my ass beat; slipping up cost too much. I was very disappointed, and kept my head down as I walked away. I took the packet to my room and lay down on my bed. Looking at everything made my stomach hurt so bad. Those things looked almost unreal to me. Looking at the prizes made me sad, too, because I knew that the chances of actually getting any were slim to zero. Just then my mother went downstairs. I barely gave her two minutes to sip her already brewed black coffee. "Mom, Mom, look at this. It's a fundraiser for school! There are so many things! Maybe could we please, please, please just get one thing?" I asked, pointing at the peanut brittle. It looked like it was jumping off of that page at us. Closing the book and looking at me she said, "No. You know that we can barely keep the hot water on, and I have no time to help. It's not going to happen honey." *Honey? How dare her*, I thought. She was trying to be sweet, and she had just crushed me. Theo heard our conversation, and as always he had to butt in. "Now you know that for you to even ask is bull crap when you know damn well that we can't. You are so selfish, Jaycee!" I looked at my mother for help, but she left me there hanging as always, so I flipped. "Selfish? You want to talk about selfish? Ok, how about you, Theo, getting the hot water shut off because you spend all of your money on partying?" The words flew out; "So fuck you!" He lunged after me and my legs stumbled up the stairs, but he was too fast. He got me. He was ripping his belt off as I fought as hard as I could, but he was too strong. He had my pants down and the beating began. He kept saying, "If you want to talk like an adult, then you're getting beat like one!" When he was done I was hyperventilating and throwing up. He knew enough was enough, I guess, because he left. Hour's later not even hunger mattered to me. I hated everything; life, my family, even my mother. Hate boiled inside of me, and my spirit was broken. Getting that upset both physically and mentally scared that crap out of me. Who was I becoming? To use such foul language was a first, but I knew exactly where I had learned it; Theo. Once, when we were on one of our trips back from Pennsylvania, he and my mother were arguing. He always talked to my mother like shit. I had no idea why she put up with it. I would never want to be with a guy with a disgusting mouth like that, ever. Anyway, he had been swearing again and she yelled at him to stop. He kept going, and he said the word "fuck" sixty-seven times in front of us kids, over and over, just to spite her. My ears burned with that word and hurt from the yelling. My mother was so angry that she said the word I had always hoped to hear; divorce. But filling with joy was a complete and utter waste of time, because when I told her that we didn't need a mean guy and that we would be fine, she jumped to his defense. I felt that him beating my ass for saying a word that he liked so much was a little unjust.

Sitting in my room all night did give me a great idea, though. An idea that was bound to work out for me…it had to! "Screw them", I thought. If I want to do a fundraiser, I'm going to do it myself. They didn't have to know, and I didn't want a dime from them either. Waiting for the right time to ask for my freedom back from Theo was my next big challenge. Timing was key. I slowly crept down the stairs; I had to be careful of every move that I made, considering the fine line that I had already been walking. It seemed like every stair was creaking and cracking, and the noise was magnified times ten in my head, so loud that it hurt. It almost pained me to take another step, but no. Not this time. This was my quest, and I was not going to be stopped by my own fear. He was watching football, and he was as sucked in as usual. He loved television; it was his Achilles heel, and yet another downfall. It was annoying, because trying to get through to him when the T.V. was on was like talking to a brick wall. The feeling of being a pest bothered me. Why couldn't anything be simple? Maybe I was the one who couldn't talk to my parents the way that they needed me to. Standing to the side of the chair that he was reclined in, staring at my shoes with my hands behind my back, it was almost impossible to get a word out, but I did.

"Can I go outside?"

"Did you learn your lesson?"

"Yes."

"Is your room clean?"

"Let me check."

I ran upstairs as fast as I possibly could, quickly shoving things under the bed and into my drawers. There was no time for anything else. I almost forgot to shove the fundraiser down the back of my shirt.

Then I went flying down the stairs and out the door, leaping because I was free! Theo was yelling after me to check about my room, but at that point it didn't matter, because my feet had already taken me far away from his voice.

The streets were empty and quiet, and the air was dead and had an eerie quality to it. For some reason in my neighborhood, children were sparse. The pavement sounded loud under my sneakers. With the dark clouds and lack of sound, it felt like Elm street just where was Freddy waiting? My stomach was getting tight. When I got to the first house, it was an old, greenish color, and you could tell that whoever lived there really had no desire to take care of the house or yard. When a little old white haired woman answered the door it made perfect sense to me. She was shy and kind and she looked at the pamphlet, and without even realizing it I was directing her to buy peanut brittle. She said that she wasn't sure her teeth would allow her this pleasure, as they were faux. The disappointment stunk, and she wound up getting some peanut butter clusters for her grandchildren, but nonetheless, a sale was a sale. I moved on, careful not to choose any houses where the people might tell my parents what I was up to, which made for slim pickings. Being alone was a feeling that had become all too familiar; it was normal, but it hurt. It hurt because I deserved a person, someone who would understand me fully and love me. It was that day on that walk that I realized that somewhere out there, whether it be a boy or a girl, there had to be at least one person that would love and understand me for me, and only me. Eventually there was an older man who purchased the peanut brittle, and my mission was accomplished! Forget about the big prizes; the real prize was that I had done something big by myself. Until I ate all of the peanut brittle, chocolate turtles, and tub of cheese popcorn the week they were given out, that is to celebrate! But then the school called my house. Shit! I was grounded for a month.

What happened next was very unexpected. Our teacher had schemed up a project idea in her head for history, but in order to do it we were going to need to be paired up with a partner. My underarms began to sweat. As Mrs. Beavers made her pairings, I couldn't help but feel like the black sheep, because the numbers were dwindling. It also didn't help that stupid Ariel said, "I sure hope I don't get paired up with someone who smells or is ugly!" Ugh. I rolled my eyes. What a bitch! Plus, I'd rather die than be partnered with that evil thing. Even Mrs. Beavers looked irritated with her, so at least I wasn't alone. I cocked my head and gave that bitch a look that held enough spite in it to last me for the rest of the fifth grade school year. Victory was finally mine. She had pissed off the teacher, the one person you never want to let down. Mrs. Beavers was so annoyed she told her to go to the principles office and wait until further notice. I was thrilled! She really melted my heart, and having her as my fifth grade teacher was one of the best things that had ever happened to me. When she called my name I almost flipped over in my desk. Then she called her name; Ashland Lomax. I turned in my seat to look. There she was, smiling ear to ear at me, and I was doing the same. Ashland was a cute little black girl with a smile for days! I was so happy that she was my partner. I walked over to her and gave her a compliment on her tri-colored sweater that her mother had obviously picked out. Her voice squeaked when she talked, but I loved it. It was different. She was different, just like me. We were a perfect match! We exchanged numbers so that we could plan to do our project. That night the phone rang. I almost tripped going down the stairs, and sure enough, on the other end was that squeaky, raspy voice that belonged to Ashland. We talked for an hour. The next day we united and it was like we never parted. I felt pure joy in seeing her, and that smile melted me even more now. We barely talked about our project; everything but, in fact. We just found interest in so many other things! Her mother had suggested that I sleep over, and that a visit to the local library was in order, as long as it was okay with my mom. This was the best news! Ashland and I jumped up and down in excitement, because there was nothing more that either of us wanted to do than just be together. Friday couldn't come fast enough! I pretty much avoided anything at home or around it that would destroy my newfound happiness. Selfishly, I just wanted to ride the wave as long as I could. Bumping into him even once was all I needed to knock the wind right out of my sails. But he caught me, and there was no way to escape. My stomach hurt so badly afterwards. His hands hurt me. Once I was out of his grasp, Friday was my only focus. Making it through the day was hard; it felt like school was taking forever to end. The excitement of knowing that the day would be even longer together made our faces gleam. When she came in and I showed her around, her mom talked to my parents. I was kind of embarrassed because our house was less than impressive. In fact, it was actually gross. But since I had run around for the past three hours cleaning my ass off, it wasn't as bad as usual. As I was showing her around she flung her arm over my shoulder, and as we were walking, Oreo attacked her. "AHHH!" We screamed, and her mother came running. He nipped her, and Theo took the still-attacking dog away. We were unsure of why he did that. Was he protecting me? Or was it the color of her skin? I didn't care, because either way it pained me to see my new buddy scared like that. Now it was definitely time to go, and I wouldn't blame her mother if any future sleepover would have to be at her house from here on out. That dumb dog didn't know a real attacker when he saw one. Why couldn't he chomp on Len? He put his hands on me.

Ashland's mom was very proper. You could tell that she was a woman of the church, although I didn't think the catholic one. She had a strict look, and she sat so stiffly that it made me nervous. Ashland's parents were separated, and it was clear that her mother was the commander and chief. Her father was in the navy, so he wasn't around much, and I could tell that it bothered her when she talked about it. I felt bad for her, because she truly only deserved the best. I could see her mother watching me in the rearview, judging me, and it hurt. Knowing exactly what she was thinking made me feel like even less than the poor, white girl I was. Then she asked me what I liked to do for fun. I gave her a very shy and quiet response; "Play outside." She said that was good, and I thought, *if you only knew that I let a monster play with me, you would never let your daughter see me again.* Wishing that she would like me wasn't going to change the fact that she had already judged me, so Ash was my only concern. We giggled in the backseat a while, and then Ash asked me what kind of music I liked. I told her I liked MC Hammer, Vanilla Ice, Boyz II Men, but that my favorite was New Kids On The Block; I even had all the dolls! She giggled, agreed with all of my choices, and asked her mom to pop in the Body Guard tape. The music played, and what happened next was magic. She lit up like a Christmas tree, so bright and shiny. What a joy this girl was! She sang the words, "and I will always love you." She pointed at me, and then kept singing the next verses. She knew every word, and when the song was finished she said her name; the great Whitney Houston, and at that moment I knew that I was in love.

That night her mother ordered cheese pizza. It was wonderful. Two slices filled up my empty belly, and then we retreated to her small bedroom in her mothers small, clean, two bedroom apartment. We lay there talking and laughing all night long. I went over to my bag to get my socks because my feet were cold, and it was then that I saw a rock-sized lump stuck to the bottom of my sock. We looked at each other, puzzled. Then we smelled it and realized what it was. Ash said it first; cat poop! A wave of humiliation came over me, but before a word could leave my lips she lost it! She fell back onto the bed laughing so hard that it made me laugh! We were crying from laughing so hard; it was difficult to even breathe! We woke up her mother, though, so we did get into a bit of trouble. It was one a.m. so I could understand, but that still didn't stop Ash. Her favorite thing to do was laugh, and I enjoyed seeing her do it! Ash and I would be friends forever, I was sure of it.

When we were at school we were inseparable, and it was the best feeling. Nothing compared to it, except my grandmas love, of course. One day when I got to school, Ash's desk was empty. I was confused and disappointed, assuming that my poor friend was sick and that I would have to give her a call later to check on her. Later that night, I didn't have to call her; she called me first. I was glad, because worry didn't even describe how I felt about not knowing where she was. Her bubbly voice was low and sad, and what she said next ripped both of our hearts right out of our chests. "We have to move. My mother can't afford to live up here without family, so we have to move back down south." The tears streamed down my hot, pink cheeks, and I could hear her sobbing, too. All I could do was arrange one last meeting, because a week was all that we had. Seeing her beautiful face was all that I could think of that day, and waiting to go get her was taking forever. Time was at a stand still until we met, and then it flew by! We were so upset! Couldn't there be another way? I begged and pleaded, but we both knew the answer, and I felt so selfish to even ask her, but I had to try. We both exchanged gifts. I had written her a long note expressing the love and friendship I felt towards her in such a small time, and how I couldn't understand or explain our connection. She had shown me true friendship, and that would never be forgotten. I also gave her the stuffed teddy from my room that she had always liked. Her gift to me was a homemade blank tape with hearts on it. We hugged and parted ways, knowing that this would be the last time that we would ever see each other in this lifetime again. The car ride was silence, and I was glad that Theo kept a lid on it for once. He could tell that I was hurt, so he was kind to me, and I would remember this. I ran up to my room and dove face first into my pillows. There weren't tears, but waterworks, and the pain kept me curled up in a ball for hours. When Erick passed by me he knew that the pain was too much to bear, so he left me there to grieve. After the sun went down, the tears finally stopped. A hot shower and some chicken noodle soup seemed to be my best bet. I went through the motions slowly. Even putting the soup into the bowl hurt. Before anyone could bother me I took my shower and went back up stairs. Even though the shower had cleaned me, the salt from my tears still lingered. My next move was one that probably should have waited, but I couldn't. I was truly yearning for any part of her so I got the tape. I slid it into the old boom box I had gotten years ago and waited. Then there she was in her giggly, raspy voice that had melted me from the very beginning. "Jay, I wanted you to know, silly girl, that even though we are both sad right now and we will be so far apart, I will always love you!" There was a pause, and then, boom, the song played and I was at sea again. There were so many thoughts that wouldn't stop running through my stupid head. It was hard to stop the memories. They were so good that it made the pain ten times stronger and that song was killing me, ripping out my insides, but I still hit rewind over and over and over until I fell asleep with her school picture by my bed.

As that year passed, things kept changing. I was changing, growing, and becoming more of a person. My feeling towards life, as well as my desires, were stronger now, and any doubts that I had ever had about Len doing bad things to me were about to come crashing into my face like a ton of bricks. One day in school our teachers called us to an assembly. We all loved those because it cut our math class time short, and for me there was nothing better than that. This also gave us a chance to see our friends and the rest of the school. A few police officers were standing center stage, waiting for us all to get situated and quiet. We all knew the local police, especially me, because we had to take D.A.R.E. (Drug Abuse Resistance Education). But I knew them because one was my uncle. Kay Lockmond was the chief. When I saw him, I kind of just knew that it probably wasn't a good thing, since he was usually tied up with city problems and real criminals. Before he spoke, he gave me a wink, and that made me nervous because all of the other kids were watching. I didn't know if you earned any cool points for that, so I kept it to no reaction at all. "Hello, today we are here about a very serious matter; sexual abuse and child molestation," he began. The sweat began to pour from my underarms and the top of my head, and then my brain asked, *what the hell did he just say? What are the words he said? Pay attention and wake up!* I knew I needed to pull myself together right away. Uncle Kay talked about how people should touch each other. He called it red light and green light touching, and at that very moment the room became empty. The other kids all seemed to disappear, and the spotlight was on me. I had one thought; *that son of a bitch!* I was frozen, but I didn't really have one single feeling. The words that the officers spoke played like a broken record in my mind, over and over again. I had a feeling of guilt, as if my uncle was going to have the officers come arrest me because he knew that out of all of the kids there, I knew something about this awful crime. I looked around the room as if the other kids knew it was me, and it was all too much. My uncle said that if we needed to tell we could, and not to be afraid, but I knew better. Imagine what embarrassment and hurt I would cause him and our family. I knew from that very moment that this was my mess and the only way to get out was going to be on my own.

When something becomes frozen the way that my mind did, it's hard to chip away at the solid ice block that forms; after too long the freezer burn sets in, and soon it's all garbage. Hiding was the best thing for me then, or the safest anyway. That way he couldn't get to me, and neither could my parents, which gave my mind time to thaw. The first few days were the hardest, because the nightmares that he had caused me were painful. He had been torturing me for years, and doing it behind my mothers back made it even worse, because I felt guilty about it. It made me sick in every way, and every part of my body was in pain. Nothing could undo the awful things that he had done to me. Nothing at all. I knew one thing for sure; never again would he put his putrid, disgusting hands on my body, or I would scream bloody murder. That was a guarantee. My anger grew the more that I sat and stewed about it. He was a bastard, and the most horrible images flowed through my mind about his justice. Should he be hanged like people were in the past, since I was just a child? No, that was too old fashioned. Jail for the rest of his life, perhaps? I knew one thing; telling anyone was out of the question. The humiliation was too much for me to handle. To expose this about an already broken family would only make things worse. Besides, I could never hurt my mother like that. She had been through enough. I kept looking out my window and checking, not to see if he was there, (he was always there), but to check and see if the sun would allow enough time to run to a friends house or ride my bike away from my house. Everything that I did now was very careful because getting caught was not an option. My luck may have been running short, though, because that night fear ran through my veins.

The day went ok, with nothing unusual about it. It was a Friday night and I had opted not to go to my grandmothers because my girl friends Heather and Rainanne wanted to hang out, and that sounded like a good idea. They wanted to eat pizza and talk about boys. I hadn't really thought about boys, because with my situation I didn't really have time. We sat in a circle on Heather's bedroom floor playing the dream phone game, calling all of the hot guys on the board, and then Rain had an idea; "Hey Jaycee, why don't you call Randy, Shannon's older brother? He's totally crushing on you!" My cheeks turned red and I told her to shut it! "What are you talking about? Seriously, you're not even funny to joke." I was annoyed. "No Jay, I swear," she said. "I saw him at Erick's game and he was totally checking you out! So are you going to call, because we kind of told him you would." What?! I looked at them for a moment and then it dawned on me; he was kind of cute. "Duh!" they shouted. "Now call!" Before I could even move, there was a young, male voice on the other end of the real telephone.

The date had been set up and it still really hadn't sunk in that a boy actually wanted to date me. He wasn't really as shy as I thought he would be, but that may have had something to do with the three year age gap; he was fourteen, but he had just had his birthday so it wasn't that bad, I thought. My girlfriends didn't seem to have a problem with it at all, and neither did his younger sister, Shannon. Shannon was going to set up a sleepover so that Randy and I could have our date. The truth was that Shannon and I were just acquaintances, so he must have really liked me to get her to do that. She was two years older than me, so we only really knew each other from going to our brother's baseball games. Now that the plan had been set there was no way out. The truth was that no matter what my nerves told me, it was going to happen; my first date!

When I got home that night at about eight p.m. I was feeling pretty great, and a nice hot shower and sleep were in order. My mother had been at the bar so she was a bit sloppy, and Theo was watching T.V., so I went up to my room. Good thing, because his signature knock was banging on the door. My back stiffened straight and that sick feeling washed over me, as well as feelings of hate and anger. I passed the time by pacing the floor and doing things that made zero sense until I thought that he was finally gone. Hearing that wicked voice when he spoke made me want to put my hands right over my ears, because there were no words that he could ever say to anyone that would be worth listening to, ever. After about ten minutes or so my mother called my name. I acted like she never called me, but that plan backfired. Her second attempt was even louder, and this time she called me down. Shit, I was screwed. I had to think quickly. "Yeah, Ma?" She said that Len was here and wanted to say hi, and to come downstairs. I said no thanks, and told her that I was too tired and going to bed. "Are you sure, it's early?" I told her yes, it had been a long day. Then he tried to yell up, but I slammed the door and slid down the back until I was sitting. I pressed my head to the door, listening. I heard his tone become dark and he told my mom that I had been awfully rude and that she should watch me closer. Then I heard her jump to my defense! My ears perked up. "Look, my daughter is tired, Len, and if she doesn't want to be bothered then you have no right to take it personally. It's her age." Go mom! I was so happy, and it worked too. That bastard stormed off. With a sigh of relief, a peaceful calm came over my bones and my room regained balance. Had I heard her calling me down again? I slowly crept down the steps and stopped about half way. Theo was watching "The Color Purple" with Oprah Winfrey. I peered around to watch, and what I saw was not what I had expected. This movie was about forced rape and sexual abuse! I saw women being beaten by colored men and my anger was growing. I didn't even want to look at the horror anymore, and apparently I didn't have to because my mother had another conversation with Theo in mind. Thankfully Theo turned off the movie. Mom was drunk, so she never even heard me come down. The words she spoke next sent shockwaves down my spine. "Do you think that Len is touching Jaycee? It was awfully strange for him to come over here like that, and she has been acting so off lately, hiding in her room all the time. Do you think he's being funny, because when I was younger my grandfather used to molest me, and I never told anyone." Theo said that he'd better not be, or he'd go right over and smash his glasses into his face right now! Then he asked my mom if she should ask me. Just like that I knew it was time to go downstairs and face the music. Slumping was my usual position, but not at this moment. Right then I was stiff and uncomfortable, but my mother was too drunk to tell. This was one time that I was thankful for that, because if she wasn't, who knows if she would have picked up on the fact that any answer given was going to be far from the truth. Her words were like knives in my body, every question was about the harsh reality that was my truth. It hurt so badly, and the fact that she knew of the dirty secret was the most painful thing, all from just a five-minute conversation. "No, no, no. Yes, mom, I would tell you," was all that I could get out before I pleaded with her to free me from her alcohol-fueled sermon. Her honesty was pure, but her delivery was brutal. I flew up the stairs but stopped dead to peek over the rails so that I could hear the rest of their conversation. "Theo, do you think she's ok?" He said, "I'm pretty sure she is. She's smart, Jean, now let it go." Wow, I thought. He bought it! Did I really manage to avoid the situation for now? Would it be enough to calm my mother was the real question, because there wasn't going to be very much room for lies now that she suspected the truth. There was no way that sleep was going to happen, and since tomorrow was Saturday and I could sleep all day, I decided to melt a box of crayons for old time sake. As my rainbows flowed, so did my mind. How was I going to avoid him? Well, on the weekends laying low at grandmas was going to be my best bet. Then during the week I had school and I could sneak out the back over the rock wall to get to my friends houses. When my mom wanted to go to the bar I would beg her to stay, and if she wouldn't then grandma could pick me up or I could sleep over at a friends house, so I had all the hours of my days covered. But even having my days mapped out didn't feel like enough. Nothing would ever feel like enough if I was living like this, always on the run with no peace. For once in my life I wished that I could move far away, just like Ashland and start over. It was then in that moment my brilliant brain had hatched a plan.

I must have needed rest, because I damn near slept until noon on Saturday. The phone rang and it was grandma. She asked to pick me up, and it was just the get away that I needed. Grandma always knew when to swoop in and save her girl. We went to lunch and went shopping and to church, which was extremely boring but so safe, and we even got to have ice cream after. The next day we took a ride up to Sandwich and took Gram to do all of her errands. She always had good life advice, too. Gram encouraged the Catholic faith and the right up bringing, and as I grew up it made more and more sense. We loved her Polish cooking, but now she was getting into her early nineties and she really needed us to help more, so we did. She and grandma fought less, which was nice, because even grandma knew that time wasn't going to slow down for her mother. Those visits were the best, and by the end we could only feel happy and content. Feeling refreshed and rested from my weekend was exactly what I needed, because it was time to break the news to my parents that we were going to be moving soon. How they were going to take it was going to require a certain amount of energy and strength.

They sat in the kitchen, slowly drinking their morning coffee. My tiny body crept near. My nerves were setting in until I heard them talking about bills and how bad things were getting and I knew that this was the moment to strike. I slithered into the kitchen like a dirty snake, which I pretty much was at this point, but what choice did I have? My survival was at hand. It all blurted out like verbal vomit; "Why don't we just move?" They just stopped and stared at me. Now I might really vomit. "Jaycee," Theo began. "It's not that easy, but it's not looking good as far as staying here, either." I was floored, my jaw hanging. *Say something,* I thought. *Don't blow this opportunity!* I was just standing there like a jerk. "Too bad we can't just move to Pennsylvania and live next to Gram and Pap…" Theo replied with, "Jaycee, if we move anywhere it's going to be around here, because this is where the shipyard and my job are." "Oh, well can it be to near Grandma? Anywhere but Middletown!" I pleaded. They told me that was enough and to go away, as if my opinion was garbage to be tossed to the side. I hid on the side of the stairs as always and took my spy position. Being able to hear their voices as if I was still in the kitchen made me feel like I was a part of their big decision; even if I didn't have a say, I felt that I had to right to listen in. "Jean, what about those apartments in Portsmouth? The area's not the greatest and the schools are just ok, but the place is in our price range and we could move within the month." At first my mother seemed unsure, but Theo kept pushing and seemed to have his mind made up.

The truth was that whether we moved to Alaska or Portsmouth, I was a victor! The success of my plan had far exceeded my expectations. I had been yearning and hoping that it would work, and my dream was coming true. I could have a new start, a fresh beginning, a do over. The joy and excitement I felt couldn't be put into words. It would have killed me to try and sum it up, so for once I just enjoyed it; this was mine and no one could take it from me. This was probably the one and only time that I would be so grateful to Theo. His decision to move three towns over was going to save my life. It dawned on me that the only reason that we were moving was because of the financial mess that we were in and not because they would have actually taken my request into consideration, but it didn't matter to me; my freedom was more important. That night lying in bed at that house was by far the best night of my life.

The more my parents talked about moving the more sure I was that the word would spread and that he would catch wind and come storming over, and sure enough he did. He tried to persuade my mother not to be so hasty and to think about what was best for the children. Now, I'm no expert, but I'm pretty sure that one thing that you should never do is tell a mother of two is what is best for her children. I was right; she lost it! "Don't you tell me what is best for my family. I understand that you're upset, but we don't have a damn choice, Lennon! Now, you can go, because quite frankly we don't give a shit what you think about our life choices." She held open the door. I made sure that he saw my peeking, smiling face, which only outraged him more. This pleased me greatly. Mother, one, son of a bitch, zero! I gained a new level of respect for my mother. I decided to start packing my things to be helpful. A few hours passed and a phone call interrupted my delightful packing process. Mom called me downstairs. It was a phone call that would change my life forever. On the other end of the line was Shannon, Randy's sister, from down the road. I guess she wanted to know if we were still on for our sleepover, which had been arranged by none other than Rainanne and Heather. Ugh, those bitches! "Yeah sure, I'll be there. What time?" She told me four-thirty and hung up. I explained to my mother that she had invited me for a sleepover, which wasn't a problem because it was essentially a free sitter for an evening. It was a win-win for everyone, I guess. My nerves were pretty shot for the rest of the day. The idea of hanging out with a strange boy for so many hours wasn't exactly a comfortable thing for my stomach to handle. Just the thought that we didn't know each other already made me feel awkward. What if we didn't even get along? *Boys are really starting to make growing up tricky* I thought as I walked as slowly as possible to Shannon's house a few blocks over. Wondering what they felt and thought puzzled me. They hate you when you're young, they make fun of you while you're growing up and are awkward, and then all of a sudden they want to date you. What was this? It dawned on me as I stepped on the lawn and looked up at him smiling at me that I was about to find out.

I picked my head up, which had been staring at my pink converse sneakers, when he spoke. It seemed simple enough; after all, this was our introduction. "Hey, how's it going?" he asked in the most cute, casual voice, and he had me. Shit. He grew on me by the second, and every word that he said was cool. There were feelings inside of me that were growing that I hadn't even know were there before. He wanted to take a walk and I agreed. At first he was shy and quiet, but that faded quickly because the more time we spent together the more we realized that we were a natural fit and that we both wanted the same thing; each other. He was tall but he didn't tower over me. It was a good height. There was a bit of chub on his stomach, just enough to see it jiggle when he laughed, but that was fine. He had adorable, straight hair cut into the popular bowl cut. This kid was cute! His most attractive feature was his cheeks. When something happened to get him nervous those cheeks grew huge, dark pink circles around them, and it drove me nuts! It was so cute, and I had never seen this happen to a boy before. The first time I saw those rosy-reds was in the woods that very day when we were walking side by side and my clumsy feet got in the way beneath me. I stumbled and he grabbed my hand to pick me up. I looked into those dark blue eyes. His cheeks went nuts and so did I. It was funny; if I didn't know any better I would think that he had been waiting for this perfect opportunity to happen, because he never let go of my hand. Just this once I was glad that my long, clumsy legs were so inconvenient. He asked me if I wanted any food, and the truth was that I was starving, but being too shy to tell him I said "Not really," and he looked bummed. I knew that he didn't like my response, so I suggested that we go back to the house so that I could use the restroom, and that was a huge relief to both of us. When we got back we saw that Shannon had ordered pizza, and we were both thrilled to be eating. A few other friends were showing up as well. He gave me a smile now and then, and that made me feel calm. I was still "in", and the night would probably only get better from here on out. He ate like a teenage boy; a lot! Growing boys needed the fuel, I thought. When we were done Shannon suggested that we all go outside and play a giant game of "manhunt", and everyone was down for that. She threw in one last detail as we ran out the door; girls vs. boys! Randy looked at his sister with an expression that said "Seriously?!", but she just ran by and gave his arm a punch as she grabbed me by the elbow and pulled me away. "Say goodbye, love birds!" she shouted. My fingers were still warm from holding his hand as we slipped into the darkness. My heart was racing, pounding so hard in my ears that I couldn't even take it! The waiting, the darkness, the silence other than the scream of a capture in the distance; it was nerve-wracking. I was nervous because Shannon had run off with her boyfriend, leaving me alone with the unknown, which I hated. But it didn't matter for long, because just then it was game over for me. The smell of his breath made me dizzy; it was sweet, like peppermint. "Hey, hot stuff," he whispered as he crouched down next to me. An instant wave gushed through my body; it was lust. He was just so sexy at that moment. "Don't worry, babe, stick with me an you'll be safe. We can win this thing!" When he held my hand and pulled me through the woods I felt like I was floating, and I couldn't help but think about the "babe" thing. What was that? Did he mean...could he really think that we were going to be more? The thought twisted me up inside; for once the universe was on my side! He stopped to ask me if I was ok about ten times, which was sweet, and the final time we sat with our backs against a huge tree. It seemed like the perfect moment. Closing in on his face, I saw his cheeks turn red. I couldn't help it; I had every intention of kissing his lips, but the cheek seemed like a better option. It was warm and soft, and he seemed pleased by this gesture when I opened my eyes. If only time wasn't against us! We had to run again, now because we saw base and no one was in sight! We won! The others made fun of us, calling us "love birds" and being sore losers. We knew the real reason for our epic win; we wanted it! When we were getting cleaned up and into our sweats, Shannon asked me how it was going with Randy. But before I could even answer she warned me that he was a sweetheart, and that whatever he was feeling was genuine. It surprised me that she would question the motives of his much-younger date, but I could see why. He was the real deal. To relax her I let her know that my feelings were real too, and that was the truth. Mention of his name sent a signal straight to my heart, and she must have known that because the conversation ended there.

That smile could brighten up any room, and that's exactly what happened when I walked in. The room was set up for some movie that they all wanted to watch, but his smile brightened the darkness. He patted the open seat next to him with an open arm, and that was enough of an invitation for me. We both had the chance to freshen up, and he must have put on cologne or something, because that hot, sweaty smell of manhunt had disappeared, and was replaced with a rainforest-musk smell, which I thoroughly enjoyed as he pulled me closer.

"Hey, do you like scary movies, babe?" (There it was again!)

"It depends, how scary?" I was concerned.

"Scary enough for me to hold you nice and close?"

"Ok, well in that case, Freddy-Kruger me away!"

He laughed out loud and squeezed me with his long, boyish arms. At this point my behavior had really begun to please me. It was like I had become funny, mature, and witty, all rolled into one pretty girl. Could this get any better? *Shut up stupid, don't jinx it like you always do!* I thought. Over-thinking was my worst quality. Well, not tonight and not with him! I had to just let it be easy. Quickly my mind was shut down, though, because a new horror was before my eyes; one only a really sick mind could think up.

The man in the all-black-leather mask and chain-suit chased the little black boy all through the halls of his creepy house, and my eyeballs were glued. There was a disgusting rottweiler dog that was trained to abuse, and it was a beast! Killer was his name, and there was nothing stopping this insane creature. A girl who lived in the house and was badly abused by her parents helped the boy try to escape through the walls. Inside of the walls there was another abused boy with his tongue cut out. He looked dead, but really he wasn't. Guns shots rang out as the psycho yelled, "I'll get you, nigger!" That probably bothered me the most. The mother was an evil, rotten, prejudice person too, and when she used that word it made me cringe. Randy kept asking if I was ok, or if I needed anything. He was really the only reason that I stayed. When I saw murder, that was it. My stomach became sick. There were people under the stairs who were abused so badly that it was terrifying. The name of the movie fit perfectly, and it was one that I would never forget; "The People Under The Stairs". It was the first Wes Craven film that I had ever seen, and hopefully it would be my last; the value of sleep did mean something to me! He grabbed me around the waste and said, "Wasn't that so awesome? You weren't afraid, were you babe?" He must have known the answer to that! At least, I thought he did, but I figured that I better play it cool just incase. "Boy, I felt you shaking more than me!" I joked. We looked at each other and laughed a lot. It was nice that we were having little moments together. Just then Shan made an announcement; "Whoever is tired can stay down here and sleep." She paused to see who was lame enough to accept that invitation, and when no one did she nodded and signaled all eight of us attending the party to follow. We all wondered what this girl was up to as she directed us to sit in a large circle on her bedroom floor. You could tell by everyone's antsy bodies that no one knew what the circle was for; not even her BFF or boyfriend, who wore the same blank expression as the rest of us.

Shannon was tall and thin with super cute short, wavy hair. Everything about her was mature and she was in command of everything that she did. Her style was her own; tight pants and half-cut tops that showed off her perfect belly button. She wore converse sneakers with neon paint splatters and the laces tied right up to the top. But what I liked most about her was that she didn't care what others thought. She was her, take it or leave it, she didn't care. She was the girl that I longed to be. She stood in the middle of the circle, modeling a bottle of coke. She showed it to everyone and then said, "My game, my rules. Everyone agree?" A couple people asked what game, and a few said that it better not be anything gross, but other than that everyone agreed. She was good like that. She took the biggest guzzle of soda that I had ever seen a girl take. She was really into it, she tilted her head as far back as she could and drank. I thought she would go for the finish! When she was done she passed the bottle and everyone drank from it until it was gone. Soda wasn't my thing at all; in fact, I hated it. When the soda was gone she sat the empty bottle in the middle of the circle and then sat down with us, now our equal. "Now," she said. "Who wants to go first?" First? What the heck was she talking about? "Older brother," she called. "You go; you're the love bird, after all." He looked at me, then around the room, and everyone looked back at him. He leaned in my ear and whispered, "Don't worry, if it lands on anyone else, I'll barely play." He looked serious. Now I was nervous, because I wanted to know what the hell we were playing! The fact that Randy was an expert at this game bothered me. Maybe hanging around with an older crowd would bite me in the ass after all. As he got up he placed his hand on my shoulder as if to assure me that everything was going to be ok. But was it? He got up and went to the middle of the circle, placing his hand on the bottle and never taking his eyes off of me. His grip was so tight that the snap the bottle made when he released it made me jump. It echoed through the room. It spun so hard that it must have gone around thirty times until it finally started to slow down. As it slowed, so did time, and my eyes never left the bottle until it stopped. My eyes looked up, searching for his, and when they met he leaped across the circle, took me and swept me away with his lips! Our lips glided together and his mouth on mine was perfect, my head, body, mind, legs, and spirit were spinning. We were spinning together! When my eyes opened I needed to take a step back to get some control of myself; I just wanted to grab him again. We looked into each other's eyes and knew that would be the kiss we would never forget. His eyes looked different after that kiss, almost wild, and I was glad to see that because then I would never have to question what happened between us that night. We could see on everyone's face how eager we had made them to get their kisses, but we had set the bar pretty high, I thought. Every time that thing spun my heart hoped that it would happen again, but it didn't. We each painfully had to kiss other people, but not like we had kissed each other. The others were respectful of that. Once, Randy got called out for being too cheap by trying to cheek-kiss, and I think that he had wanted me to do the same, but there was no way; rules are rules. It was driving him absolutely nuts, sitting there and watching his girl get kissed, but it didn't bother me one bit. I'm not sure if it was just because I wasn't the jealous type or because I knew that I already had his heart and that none of the other girls mattered. His obvious displays of discomfort were enough to make me feel secure. Randy leaned over to his sister and they whispered a few things to each other, but my confidence was up so I didn't feel uncomfortable about it. Just then Shan stood up and announced that it was time to switch it up; "Truth or dare!" was what left her mouth, and the group roared. Apparently everyone's lips were a little burnt out, though, because the circle broke for a quick intermission. I stood up for a quick stretch before their return. My muscles needed it; they were stiff from a good hour of spin. I searched my bag for a bottle of water and my very-favorite, must-have, can't-live-without cherry chap stick. As soon as I was done applying it I could feel him waiting, and when I turned around he was leaning against the door, all cool-like. That didn't last long, because soon he left his position and reached for my hand. He pulled me to my feet and into his arms, wrapped his hands around my waist and pulled me in close until our lips were together again. He was the perfect gentleman; never pushy, gentle, kind, sweet, and his touch was so warm. We cuddled and kissed all night long until we fell asleep in each other's arms for about an hour. It was a comfortable experience that we both needed to have.

The morning sunrise woke us both. We couldn't help but smile. It didn't take long for me to get ready because I couldn't go without a shower for much longer and he understood. He walked me to the woods where I could cut through the path to my house. He made me like him even more for that. We stood in silence. I'm not sure if it was because we were tired, but my eyes were heavy so I could only imagine how he felt. I broke the silence quickly because I was so tired. "Ok, bye then, and thanks for last night. You're fun." I turned and walked away, but as I did he grabbed my arm and said, "No wait! Actually, I have a question for you. I was wondering if you wanted to be my girlfriend?" His cheeks went flush, and the longer it took for me to answer the more he shuffled his feet in the soggy, morning leaves. This was the one question that every girl wanted to hear out of a boy's mouth for her entire life! It was a real question, with meaning. I knew that things between us were over, though, but I didn't have the guts to smash his heart into a million pieces. I wondered why. I thought it was just fun and games, but I guess that changed for him. There was something that he wanted more now; a girlfriend, and I knew why. The kiss. He said my name. I was taking too long and he was starting to sweat, beads dripping from his forehead. "Come here," I said, and I pulled him close. "Of course I'll be your girlfriend! But I can't promise that I'll be any good at it." The next thing I knew our lips were moving together again, and my head was spinning. It was like magic. He pulled away and wiped his lips, saying, "Well I think that you're doing a great job at it already!" When a guy says words like that with meaning it does something to your heart. Maybe it makes it bigger, makes it beat stronger and harder. I couldn't figure it out or how to explain it, but there was a little extra skip in my step and the leaves sounded extra crunchy under my feet. My smile was permanent; at least until the guilt set in.

Passing by his house to get to mine sent cold chills down my spine. I just wanted this one moment without his face to destroy it. He could ruin anything for me at any given time no matter what the situation, and realizing this stopped me dead in my tracks. These were going to be my memories someday and I was not going to let him take them; stealing was not ok! My feet turned my body around quickly, and in one swift motion the wrong direction became the right one. My stomach growled reminding me of my long overdue breakfast, so I reached into my pocket for two crumpled up dollar bills and marched straight into the universe market. I sat on the swing at the church playground, about to feast. I couldn't help but smile at this giant pickle, Skor bar, and, best of all, my new boyfriend! I took a big bite of my pickle and thought, "Screw you, Lennon Kindsay, you cannot steal my happiness!"

Later on I lay in my bed starring up at the glowing stars that had been there for years. They twinkled all around, but it wouldn't be long before that room darkened to me forever. This brought me to think about Randy. There would never be a good time to tell him about my departure, but I at least had an idea of when I would tell him. I was really scared more than sad. The attachment was minimal, but it was scary to think of hurting someone else's feelings. I could still rest easy knowing that it was all coming to an end, though. Luckily Erick had a baseball game the next morning, and Randy would be there. I had a little time to prepare.

When I got to the ball field the next morning I hit the concession stand and bought a pouch of bubblegum. Big League Chew usually cheered me up, but I knew that it couldn't today. He was playing first so I went to the bleachers to watch the game and get a last look at him in those tight pants, V-neck shirt and ball cap. He was always so focused, with his head in the game. He was the type of guy who put his heart into everything that he did, and this would get him far in life, I knew. When the game was over I respectfully waited until his friends were gone and let him come to me. He gave me a sweaty hug, and I asked him to walk to the park with me. Being with him this time was different. The atmosphere was tight. There was no flirty, happy-go-lucky couple this time, that's for sure, and we both knew it. The silence was deafening. We needed to be in a private place for this. The grass was bright green and the air was warm, so I asked him to sit down with me. Before a word even came out of my mouth, he knew. "Hey, I heard you were moving. Is that true?" he asked. I nodded. "It's cool, Jaycee, but you know it's not going to work anymore, right?" I nodded again. It was like the cat had my tongue. The poor guy deserved more than this. Finally, my lips moved. "You need to know that I had so much fun and being your girl made me really happy, but even if I wasn't moving our ages would always be far apart." Now he was the only one able to nod. Funny how that worked, I thought. We were really on the same page. The only thing left to do was give a goodbye kiss, which was brief and short with no magic and very little feeling. That was the last time that I saw the first boy who made me realize that there was more to life than fear of the opposite sex. There was beauty and magic. He opened me up, and now I wanted more.

Who knew that packing boxes could be the most exciting thing in the world? It gave me a chance to get rid of any old things and useless waste that I didn't need, and our whole family loved the idea of this. Saying goodbye to my friends was sad, but Rain and Heather had actually found out that their dads were being stationed down south, so they would be moving, too. We decided to play one last game of daytime-manhunt with the boys for old time sake, which was all fun and games until someone got hurt, and of course that someone was me. Erick; that son of a bitch! We were running and we tried hiding behind Rain's thick walkway door, and all of me got through except for my pinky. I was yelling and screaming, begging for him to get off of the door, but he kept pushing as hard as he could so that I couldn't get out until a shriek of terror left my throat. When he finally let the door open, all that was left of my pinky was a crumpled up mess. It was busted, and I sobbed all the way home, wanting to punch Erick in the nuts. On the trip to the hospital Theo felt bad for me. It showed on his face. He knew it hurt; it was crushed and so was I. The doctor took an X-ray and said that it was fractured for sure. He put this ugly splint thing on it and told me that if I took it off my finger would be bent forever, so it would be wise to follow his advice. My anger towards Erick was now fury! He did this to me! If he was a nice brother this could have been prevented, but I knew him all too well. He never knew when to stop until it was too late! Well, this time he had really crossed a line, and payback was a bitch. It was a good thing my excitement for packing was so strong, because this new gimp style finger was really going to slow me down.

The broken finger wasn't all bad, though. In a way it helped me in those last few days. It made hiding easy. I didn't really need excuses, just too much pain and needing rest. My parents never really questioned my absence, especially when he made several visits in the last few days. If he could never see my face again, that would be the best revenge! More than anything I wanted to make sure that he could never use or abuse me again; that would bring me the ultimate joy. Yes, I wanted more punishment than that for him, but not for the cost of my reputation. It was just too much embarrassment, even though a jail cell for him would have been great, and the money from suing him for emotional and physical abuse would have helped my family financially. Doing this would have only made my internal scar a tattoo for everyone to see. I had suffered enough; any more emotional trauma and I think they might have to lock me up at the state mental hospital in a padded room! Dancing with the devil was not on my to do list, but burning him and getting the hell out of this town was. It was a race against time now. The faster we packed and cleaned the faster I would be free. I pushed as hard as I could everyday to really help. I went to visit my dad before the move and tell him the great news, but of course all that he and Pauletta did was talk shit about my mother and say that she was only doing this to be spiteful, to get closer to him and make his life a living hell. As the number of cats in that house began to increase the amount of love he had for us seemed to decrease. Pauletta had grown more nervous since our last visit. She looked like she was on drugs or something, but she was just mental, I decided. It wasn't really nice of me to assume something like that without proof. I didn't have to ask her what her problem was, because the answer was crystal clear. It was our family, our existence. It freaked her out, she was afraid that we would steal even one second of his time, even just to say hi. She was a pathetic, witch of a woman. Yes, it would have been nice to spend time without the gawking queen listening in on everything that he wanted to talk about, even if all that happened to be was about my mother. Her jealousy was sickening, and his ranting about the unfairness of it all was enough for me. Telling him that I was tired seemed best. There were only a few seconds when she would be going to get her coat, and his cigarette was almost finished, so I knew that this was my only chance to at least tell him about my excitement. "Dad, at least we will be closer and we can see each other more now! I really can't wait to move, Middletown is the worst place on earth!" But all he said was, "Jaycee don't you get it? The only reason that your mother is moving is to be closer to me so that she can spy on Pauletta and I!" I told him that couldn't be true, that Portsmouth wasn't even his town, but he just went on and on about how bad this would be for him, and once again Jay and Erick were at the bottom of the barrel. Never once did he think about the positives, and it was too late because that evil witch was on her broomstick and flying out the door. The worst part of it was that as much as his ways sickened me and what he said made me want to pull my hair over my ears to drown out his selfish crying, I still loved him. How could I still love him? How many more vicious exchanges would I be able to endure between him and my mother before it broke me? My mother always told me that seeing him was my choice and that choice was becoming quite clear now.

Even though my father had me feeling really low and super crappy about our visit the day before, nothing could really get me down because it was moving day! I flung the covers back, and instead of making my bed or just leaving it a disheveled mess like I usually did, I folded my bedding up to the best of my ability and stuffed it into a box, duct taping it shut. If my tape player hadn't already been packed there would have been music on to celebrate, but oddly enough, even without any music on my body was dancing. It felt hungry and thirsty and playful and ready to take on the world. I was full of life! I raced downstairs to eat; stuffing my face seemed like a great way to gain momentum for my already fabulous morning. My spirit was rich. Even Erick got a warm welcome. I gave them each a big warm smile, one by one, cheeks full of fruit loops like a chipmunk. Theo asked me if I could go around the yard and gather the small, leftover yard toys and throw them away after I was finished eating. He probably figured it was rare to catch me this agreeable. It was like everything that I did in that house had meaning that day; putting my dish in the sink, getting dressed, and mostly going out into my yard one last time. The sun was bright and warm on my skin, matching the way that I felt until the darkness found me. The yard was very unkempt, typical Theo. This was making it extremely difficult for me to find any loose objects, keeping me out there much longer than I should have been. It was never safe out there; he was always watching. I went around back to the tree, figuring it would give me a better view to look down at the yard rather than through the tall grass as if I was on a safari hunt. This was a better view, and everything actually looked kind of pretty. I had a flash of memories from the woods, the yard. They were warm and happy with my friends and family, which was all I had ever wanted. "Thank you so much," I whispered. Feeling satisfied and ready, I lifted my head, only to see his dark shadow over the top of me. I leapt up to run, but he grabbed my arm and gave a strict warning;

"Don't! It is not wise for you to do this right now… I'm angry."

"Fine, let me go and I won't!" I said in a disrespectful manner, ripping my arm away from his vulgar grasp. "What do you want from me? I didn't do anything to you, just let me go!"

His tone grew dark and his shadow was like a large black bear, murderous and hungry. "Why are you doing this to me? How could you just move like this? Who do you think you are? This is your fault! You told your parents to do this! How could you be such a selfish little bitch?"

That's when I flew off the handle. "Listen, old man! My parents are the ones who decide to do things, and I just go along with them. But if you must know, yes! I am happy to be moving away! I can't wait to be out of this hell hole! It sucks and so do you! No, I don't care if you're upset. You're a dirty, disgusting old man who I want nothing to do with!" My cheeks were red and my temper had hit an all time high.

It was the first time that I had backed him into a corner. He looked as if he felt disrespected, but I didn't give a shit. He didn't have feelings; monsters don't feel. The look in his eyes gave me a chill and reminded me to be ready to bolt as soon as the time was right.

"You owe me, Jaycee. You need to come back to my house and pay me for all the things that you said you would."

"Owe you? I don't owe you shit! You got me those things because you said that you wanted to. Yes, they were things that I liked, but you knew that and that's your fault, not mine. So no, I don't owe you anything, old man!"

"Bullshit! You're a liar! You know that you owe me, and bad things happen to girls who lie!"

"Oh yeah? Well nothing bad is going to happen to me because I didn't do anything wrong and I'm done. You're going to live the rest of your sad, loser life alone, so fuck you. And guess what? You'll never, ever touch my body again, you disgusting old man!" This seemed like the time to run, because his temper was flaring. As I was running away, I heard him say something that I will never forget;

"Hey Jaycee, you know, you'll never grow up to be anything but a little slut and whore. Guys will do whatever they want with you because you're easy, and you'll never be anything more!"

I wholeheartedly believe that he meant every word that he said. I won't ever forget that expression that he wore on his face. I looked back at him, nodded as spitefully as I could, and with the biggest smile I could conjure up and said, "Well that's only for me to ever know, and for you to never find out!" I ran back into that house one last time, happier than I had ever been in my whole life. It was finally over.

As we drove down the driveway in that blue station wagon packed up to the brim, I stared at the big picture window that my brother had once broken with his baseball and said goodbye to all of the bad memories. My parents got divorced in that house. It was truly a dump. There was so much sadness for me there that it could never be restored in my mind. Even if it had brand new wallpaper and drapes, it would never be home. Even more importantly, it wasn't the house or the crap town, but the dangers that lurked outside the door, the evil that plagued me and stole my childhood. My desperate cry for help to God had been heard, and he truly helped me crawl out of the deep, dark hole that had become my life. The lies and pain could end. It could all just vanish now, as if it had never happened. The truth was, I really had no idea what Portsmouth had in store for me. Would it be hard to find new friends? Would I struggle in school? Would Erick still be the same exact jackass that he'd been my entire life? Would he and Theo grow tired of the abuse? Would my mother finally step up and be there for me, or would she go out more? Would this house actually be our home, or just another dumping ground? If that were the case, things would definitely have to change on my end. What about my dad? Well, we'd have to see about that. But one question really burned in the back of my mind. I couldn't help but think that he had won, at least a little bit, because I had allowed him to get in my head. Was I going to end up being wild and have all of the boy troubles that he had predicted? Would that be my fate? My heart really did not want that, but he had wished that on me and if it came true, I would be ruined! And finally, the last thing that I couldn't shake, the thought that stayed with me and pinched my brain until it ached; was I really free? Would I ever see the predator who had taken my entire childhood and haunted me for years ever again?

The Jaycee Diaries
Through the Eyes of a Child

Based on a True Story

K.C. Green

Dedicated To You, my beloved daughters and husband

There's not one day that passes by I stop thinking about how much I want the best for you. My love grows watching you! All of you are amazing, thank you for loving me and making me smile the way that you do; it's all a mother could ask. God knew how to build our family perfectly, so we owe it all to the man upstairs.

Mom, Dad and Brother

I love you so much. We weathered the storm even when it was raging. We always find a way to love each other no matter what, and that's worth something!

Sister;

You could write your own book, love! The best is yet to come. Thank you for embracing the crazy so well. Your mother would have been proud; trust me, I know it!

My Friends;

You always believe in my ideas and love me for me, even when they seem silly and crazy. But I guess that's what makes you some of the best friends I've ever had! You never judge, you love me for me, and you have always been the ones who make me feel like I am worth something. Thank you, loves! KD and LH

Musical Inspiration;

Music is so important to me; it pretty much makes up ninety-percent of who I am, so to the people who have the talent and the courage and are willing to share it with fans like myself, it means so much more than you could ever know.

> **Rascal Flatts**; _Thank you, truly._
>
> **Gavin DeGraw**; _The way that he moves my soul is something that could never be explained._
>
> **Blake Shelton**; _"God Gave Me You" is the best song ever! I love the way he thinks._
>
> **Darius Rucker**; _"This", he make me a true believer._
>
> **Florida Georgia Line**; _Thank you for being so fun and giving me a break from this to take my awesome ladies MN and TG out; told you they were hot! (Literally, it was 100 degrees out!)_

Thank You;

To the three boxes of #2 pencils, you served me well. Thank you!

To my Facebook family; I seriously love you to death and I don't even know what the world would be like without you, because we all need each other so much. If there weren't Facebook breaks, there might not be a book!

To everyone who had loved and supported me, thank you, thank you, thank you! They're not just words if you really mean them, and I really do!

To Ellen DeGeneres for making me laugh. You just get it, and one day I'm going to be on your show.

To Kids Who Are Afraid, and to Anyone In A Bad Situation;

Sometimes bad things happen to good people. It's okay to tell someone that you trust, because no matter how scared and afraid you are they can help! If you don't have someone, then find someone because your life is your voice to the world. Pray! Keep the faith, and ask God because he loves you and will always find justice for evil.

Love,

K.C. Green

P.s. There are so many different ways to be BRAVE! All you need to find is one!

THE
SPOKEN
TRUTH

MCGREGORY FREDERIQUE

BALBOA.
PRESS

A DIVISION OF HAY HOUSE

Balboa Press books may be ordered through booksellers or by contacting:

Balboa Press
A Division of Hay House
1663 Liberty Drive
Bloomington, IN 47403
www.balboapress.com
1 (877) 407-4847

Print information available on the last page.

ISBN: 978-1-5043-7172-8 (sc)
ISBN: 978-1-5043-7199-5 (e)

Balboa Press rev. date: 12/16/2016

CHAPTER 1

How You Should Treat a Woman

As a guy, I've seen a lot of good women get their hearts broken because of the men they have dealt with in their lives. The pain they cause themselves is only self-inflicted. You have a choice who enters and exits your life. It's sad but true. Here is a guide designed to help men treat a woman how she should be treated.

The first thing you should know about women are the three As. Women love *attention*, *affection*, and *appreciation*. If you don't provide those three things, you have already lost her. She'll find them from someone else. Trust me. I've been through this myself. I just don't want you to make the same mistakes I've made.

It's truly a blessing to have a beautiful woman by your side, especially if she's well educated, cooks, cleans, can sex you right, and will hold you down 24/7. Remember, guys, she doesn't have to do those things for you. Women want to feel appreciated, not disrespected.

I am not telling you what to do; I'm giving you my advice to keep the woman you love happy. I have seen a lot of guys who had good, faithful, loyal women, and these men still cheated with hoes who didn't give a damn about them. Even to this day, they regret it. Karma is a bitch. What goes around comes around. You don't need it coming back to you.

If you are currently in a relationship and she's acting moody or doesn't want to be touched, it's a red flag that means she's not happy.

She's not satisfied or is not feeling the relationship anymore. You need to step in and start making changes ASAP. If the two of you are living together and she works all day, she shouldn't have to come home and do the dishes. Ask yourself, "Is that fair to her?" The answer is no, not at all.

If you know how to cook, cook her a decent meal. Run her a bath. Make sure the bedroom is clean. Have candles lit and open a bottle of wine. Play romantic music. Make her feel special. I know for a fact that when she walks through the front door, she'll give you a look you will never forget.

When you're done with dinner, make sure you wash the plates while she gets in the tub. Treat her like a queen, not only on that day but every day. Show her that you care. Show her that you are willing to change your nasty ways. Show her that you are willing to make the relationship work. Show her that you want it more than she does. Fellas, once a woman realizes that, there is no way in hell she'll turn her back on you.

When you're done with the dishes, pick up the wine and two glasses and head for the bedroom. Continue to let the music play in the background. Enter the bathroom while she lies comfortably in the tub. Don't be shy to show her that you have a soft side (every man has a soft side, ladies). Hand her a glass. Open the wine, pour for her, stare into her beautiful eyes, and let her know that you are serious. At first she will think this is an act until you get her into the bedroom. Remember that acting like yourself is the key in any relationship. Don't try to be someone that you're not. Just show her the side of you that she never saw before.

Grab the towel and tell her to get up. Wrap the towel around her. Take her hand, walk her into the bedroom, and lay her gently on her back. Grab lotion. Make sure you hold her feet and rub them. Remember, she did just come from a long day of work. She should love that. Do it for five minutes before applying lotion over her entire body. It will probably turn her on. Continue rubbing her body and touching all the right spots. You will know you're doing a good job when you start hearing little noises escape from her mouth.

From that point on, you have full control of the situation. I recommend that you take your sweet time and enjoy the night with the woman you love.

Settling Arguments

Women love surprises. Even the littlest things will put smiles on their faces. Buy her flowers when she least expects it and watch how she gets all sweet right in front of you. I remember when I was dating my first love. We got into a huge argument over something small and didn't talk for two straight days. Don't let one little argument ruin your relationship. I repeat, do not let one little argument ruin your relationship. Don't allow what you have worked so hard to build go to waste. Don't let your pride be the reason why you end up single. Most men don't listen, and they find themselves alone.

On the third day after the fight, I decided to get up and go see her. I had to be the bigger person. Of course, I didn't go empty-handed. I brought her a dozen roses, fifteen balloons, and two teddy bears just because I wanted to. I needed help carrying everything; that's how much stuff I brought her. I didn't call her or anything. I wanted to pop up at her place to show her all the beautiful gifts I had brought her and to tell her I was sorry.

Funny thing about it was she was standing right in front of her house, talking to her uncle. When she saw me walking up, she flashed me a beautiful smile. I felt I had made the right decision to go see her. We made up and moved on.

See, guys, when you do things like that for your woman, she will always remember it, no matter if you two stay together or not. Your relationship might fade away, but the experiences you shared will remain in her memory.

When I'm out having dinner or lunch, I see a lot of women trying to have a conversation with their men, who are busy on their phones. Seriously, fellas, I find that downright disrespectful. If she takes you out to eat with her hard-earned money, and you're sitting on your phone all night while she's trying to talk to you, that tells me you don't deserve to be with her. She didn't have to take you out. She could've gone out with her girls or even another man. She chose to be with you that night, so don't be a fool and ruin it. At the end of dinner make sure you pick up the tab sometimes as well. Don't let her pay the tab all the time;

she shouldn't have to. She will feel like she's being used and taken for granted.

Some men focus on getting a woman, and once they have her, they lose focus on how to keep her. You cannot worry about other women. This will distract you from realizing the one you truly need is right in front of you. You do not want to lose her.

Who said we were perfect? We all make mistakes sometimes, but making the same mistakes too many times can cost us a lot. When you get a woman you want, be sure to treat her right. Don't treat her like shit; it doesn't make any sense at all. You wanted her. Now you got her! So now it's time to show her why she chose you to be her man. Do not be like those other men out there, thinking that their girlfriends or wives will wait on them forever. You'll be sadly mistaken. And once you realize it, it will be too late.

> I've been in many situations where I put my friends before my girlfriend. Trust me, that was the biggest mistake ever. When things weren't going well for me, she was always there. But I was young and stupid, thinking only about myself and my needs. I didn't care about her feelings or anything else. I thought being in a relationship was all about me—until I lost her. I grew up and learned from it and moved on with my life.

So, guys, become a real man and cherish her. Be that man who opens the car door for her, who pulls out the chair for her to sit down, and the man who gets up from his seat when she comes into the room. Treat her right, and she'll treat you even better. Loyalty is everything.

Cheating

Listen, if you are going to cheat, you might as well not be in a relationship with her at all. It's pointless, and you know it's a fact. No woman should be cheated on. She wants to be treated right. That's all she's asking from you. It is not too much to ask. You should be happy that she's putting up with your bullshit. Don't expect her to be faithful to you if you know damn well you are not being faithful to her. Don't expect her not to flirt with other men if you are out there flirting with other women. If you don't give, she won't give.

I know women can be complicated sometimes, but they lash out with their emotions when they've been hurt. Remember your goal is not to hurt her; your goal is to make her the happiest woman on this earth. She should replicate the same type of feelings.

The truth is some women don't like to party, get drunk, or hang out with their friends all night. Some want to stay home, watch a movie, cuddle, tell jokes, and be cared for. Not every woman is the same; keep that in mind. Sometimes guys, you have to put your pride aside and accept the fact that you're wrong. It's not called giving up, it's called *growing up.*

You impress a real woman by being honest and faithful. And you lose her respect and love with the first lie you tell. But some men would rather see the women they claim to love heartbroken instead of keeping it real.

That's called being selfish. If you don't want to be with her anymore, be a real man and call her. Set something up so you and she can sit down somewhere and discuss it as two adults. Don't send her a text message. A lot of guys have a habit of doing that. You didn't start the relationship like that, so why end it like that, right?

The best way not to get caught cheating by your woman is not to cheat at all. It makes sense, doesn't it? No woman wants a man who constantly does the same shit and says, "Sorry." After a while she's going to get fed up with hearing it from you. Believe me, you don't want that to happen. Once a woman is fed up, she's fed up for real. There's nothing you can do to change the way she feels about you. No matter what you do for her after that, she will look at you as the guy who broke her into a million pieces, who doesn't deserve her time.

When reality hits you, you'll know never to take a good woman for granted. You'll regret it in the long run. I've seen too many men pass up good women for hoes. They end up feeling low. They have to hold their heads down when they see their former girlfriends walking with other guys who treat them right. The woman you gave up for a hoe will continue to do better without you. Loyal, honest, respectful, she would have given you the world and everything in it.

So appreciate a woman while you have her. Respect her, and especially continue to make her happy. She needs hugs, kisses, a shoulder to cry on, an ear to vent to, and a chest to lie on. She needs a strong man to depend on, physically, mentally, and emotionally. Most of all, she needs to feel wanted. Treat her like you would treat your own daughter, because one day a guy will come into your daughter's life and break her heart. That will bring flashbacks of exactly what you did.

The words you never want to hear come out of your woman's mouth are "I am not happy with you anymore." At first, you'll act like you don't care. But when she starts showing she doesn't give a fuck, that's when you will know she's serious. Being heartbroken sucks big time. It takes away your happiness. It makes you give up on love and wonder if you will ever get into a relationship again.

I feel you shouldn't give up on anything in life. If you want something, you will go out there and get it. Don't sit back and let one relationship kill you. Seriously, guys. Just make sure the next time that you treat her like a queen. Do things differently.

Expect the woman you date to have her guard up initially. Most women do after getting hurt. It will take her a while to open up to you. When you see her giving you a little attitude, it doesn't mean she doesn't want to speak to you. It means she's being careful with her heart. Slowly but surely, she will open up. It doesn't happen overnight; these things take time.

A hoe could never do for you or give you what a real woman can. If you think so, you are a damn fool and will always get played like one. My best advice for every guy out there is if you have a woman who cares about you, who is willing to do anything for you, and who will even spend her last dollar on you—don't treat her like shit. You do not want to end up in the trash.

There are women out there who will only talk to you because of what you have. They'll make you look like a dumb ass, and even mess with your friends behind your back. So make the right decision and choose the right woman for you. Then treat her right—that's all she asks.

Rebound

The key to a woman's heart is not hard to find. Take the time to understand her. Women want to feel wanted in every kind of way. One thing I've learned is that women are smart as hell. Never play with a woman; she knows how to play it better than you. The woman you want won't take you seriously if you are flirting with everyone. Why should she give you the time of day, when she has plenty of other guys who do the opposite of what you do?

Not every woman deserves to be treated like a queen. Fifty percent of them have good men in their lives and still cheat, trying to find something more satisfying. But the other half deserves it all. They don't ask for anything. They are the ones who love you when you call them unexpectedly, the ones who smile when you send a morning text, the ones who love you for just being there, period.

There are too many heartbroken women out there who can't find a decent guy to be with. A lot of you guys complain about not having a good woman in your lives. It's because y'all are chasing the wrong ones.

I have no secrets myself, no lies; everything I say is the truth. But I don't want these women to think I'm this perfect guy when I'm not. I'm just perfect in my own way. Fellas, you are not alone. I used to be in the same boat as y'all because I dated a young, beautiful woman who was and still is amazing. Words can't describe her. Everything about her was perfect. We dated for two and a half years. Though we had our problems, we stuck together. No matter what happened, we were always there for each other. We didn't let anything come between us. We broke up a few times but always found ourselves back with each other a few months later. I just knew it was meant to be. We both could've moved on, but we chose not to because we were deeply in love with each other.

I kept making mistakes along the road. I gave my attention to other women instead of the person who had been there for me since day one. I kept denying her because I didn't want anyone to judge me and our relationship. I kept her as a secret, even though I knew what I was doing was 100 percent wrong. I didn't care. I was loving all the attention from other women. I let my pride and ego get the best of me. I didn't acknowledge what I had in front of me. But I knew, deep down inside, that other men realized what I did not.

In time we broke up again, so I started talking to another woman I barely knew. I kind of liked this new girl for the moment. Then my main girl and I got back together. Everything was fine until the new girl tried to come back into my life. On that day, I could've kept it real with her and told her I was back with my girlfriend, but I didn't. I still wanted to talk to her. I was being selfish. I wanted my cake and I wanted to eat it too.

My girlfriend figured out something was wrong, but she never brought it up to me. She kept it from me because she needed more facts to confront me about it. Then, on a Thursday morning, she found out about the other girl. The weekend came, and things didn't go as I expected them to. My girlfriend came over. She didn't even want to talk. I was expecting to work the situation out. She was in a rush to leave after she got her stuff together. I knew how upset she was, but she didn't give me enough time to explain everything. She wanted to go so bad, and I let her go. I shouldn't have let her go.

The biggest mistake I made on that day was jumping into another relationship that didn't even last a month. I felt stupid; I tried to replace her but it backfired on me. I knew I'd messed up, and ever since our breakup, I've been honest and loyal to myself.

Guys, it takes a real woman to make an impact on your life. She wants you to do better, achieve your goals, and become successful. All she wants from you is respect and love. If you are not ready, just leave her alone and let a real man handle her. Men need to realize that no matter how much our women nag us, stress us out, and start little arguments, it's just to get our attention. We do need them, at the end of the day. If she sticks by you after you mistreat her, she's not being stupid. She's giving you a chance to realize what you have.

Showing Respect

Some men really need to show their women respect. Why would you flirt with another woman when you have got your own woman to flirt with? Why go on dates with other women when you have your own woman to take out? Why tell another woman you miss her when you should be saying it to the one who misses you? Why text other women when you already have a good woman who can't wait to hear from you? Why try so hard to get in another woman's pants when you already have a woman who wants to do that with you? Bottom line, why be with a woman if you see no future with her, if you're not planning to be with her forever? If you know one woman isn't going to be enough for you, don't make one woman believe that she is.

It's shit like this that really messes a woman's head up. No woman wants a half-assed relationship. If you are going to be with her, be with her. Give it your all or give nothing at all. Don't give up your effort as soon as you get the woman you want. Women ask that you do not take advantage. Do not mistake her kindness for weakness. You mad? Take a walk to the park and figure out how the two of you will work things out. You upset? Call her, and she'll come to comfort you as a real woman should. You hiding anything? Tell her. She will never know how you feel if you don't express your feeling to her. No matter how upset she is, she will always be more understanding if you tell her straight up. You got trust issues? The relationship you want is never going to work if you don't meet her halfway, work with her, compromise, and make her feel comfortable. If you do those things, y'all can work it out without any drama.

Tons of men forget to realize how emotional women are. Simple words can hurt or scar a woman forever. But most of you will always remember those moments when she bent over backward to do anything for you—the moments she cried over you, stressed over you, waited on you, missed you, fought for you, changed for you, begged for you, and dropped everything for you. She tried to express herself and tried to get you to understand how she loved you.

There comes a point when she is fed up and done trying. She is through being a good woman to you because you've never appreciated anything she does for you.

Instead of acting like she's not good enough, how about you give back? Instead of taking from her, become a real man. She needs that from you when she needs your help.

But most likely, it is too late. She's done. She's letting you go, and she's serious this time. No more second or third or fourth chances. She's fed up with your bullshit. She's tired of wasting her time on a person who only cares about himself. When you see her happy with the next man, don't cry to get her back. When she was giving you chances, you took them for granted. You left her behind. You only proved that you no longer deserve any of her effort.

She changed, but you didn't. She changed for the better, and it's truly a shame you are missing everything she could've given you. She will always be a beautiful woman you will never get back.

Past Relationships

> You have to understand: women act the way they do for a reason. More than likely their behavior is due to something that happened to them in the past. They have been hurt. It's not that a woman is trying to push you away or hurt you. She doesn't realize how her behavior is perceived. She doesn't know what it feels like to be loved and to be treated the way she deserves. Women often take their negative experiences into the next relationship.

Sometimes it's hard to let go of the woman you love, but you can't hold on to someone who doesn't want to be held on to. Never let past relationships determine where your next one goes.

As a woman's partner, you shouldn't pay attention to other women. You should be too busy focusing on the woman you love. As her man, you shouldn't be in the next woman's face. There's no reason to be. You should be telling other women to stop flirting with you, and you definitely shouldn't be engaging in it. After all, you wouldn't want your girlfriend to flirt with other men.

Remember those three As: attention, affection, and appreciation. As her man, you shouldn't be thinking about your ex-girlfriend. As her man, you should in no way let another woman steal you away. As her man, you should be coming up with new ideas, tricks, and moves to impress the woman you love. Show her how much you cherish and appreciate her time, strength, and love. If you do, she will never forget what you have done for her.

Women don't forget anything. Trust me. They always remember the times you hurt them, made them cry, made them feel stressed, and made them feel weak. You need to take the time to understand them. Always keep this in mind: nothing in life will come easy.

❧ ❧

Good guys get shat on and good
women get cheated on.

CHAPTER 2

Why Relationships Don't Last

Many relationships don't work because people tend to bring their old relationship problems into their new relationships, which leads to arguments and lack of trust. You never want to start off your new relationship by fighting. I've been in many different relationships, and each one I thought would last forever. Instead, they all ended with arguments.

I took my sweet time to realize what I wanted out of a relationship. But while I slowly became unhappy, I never told the woman I was with. I was too afraid. I thought she would take it the wrong way.

In the midst of my unhappiness, I started to understand why a lot of relationships don't last. When we meet potential partners, we mess things up by pretending to be someone we are not. Some people don't keep it real on day one. The majority of the time, that is why they lose out on a good person in the end. And you have to keep it real with yourself before you can keep it real with the next person.

No one said relationships were easy. Relationships have their ups and downs—especially their downs. Sometimes it's better to let go than to hold on to something that's broken and can't be fixed. That's something you have to realize on your own. In all situations, you need to really understand what the main concern is. There's a difference between issues that can be worked on and issues that just won't go away.

Another reason relationships don't work out is because you're with wrong person. You can give your partner everything, act perfectly, and go out of your way. You can go to jail or go broke for them. But you can't fix a relationship if the other person is not right for you.

One of my friends met a pretty young lady. He described her to me. Everything about her was wonderful: eyes, lips, hair, skin color, and the way she spoke. Every single thing about her was perfect in his eyes.

But he had a feeling she was cheating on him. She usually came to his house every Friday. One Friday when she came, he knew something was wrong. He could just tell.

He called me up and asked me to come over and consult with him about it. He didn't want to confront her if she *wasn't* cheating on him. So we decided to set her up. I didn't want to; I should've minded my own business. But I couldn't stand by and see a good guy like him get hurt.

So he told me where she worked. The following day, I stopped by. I approached the lady smoothly. I knew what I was doing was wrong, but it was too late. And on that day, I learned why relationships don't last. I spoke to her for ten minutes. We exchanged numbers. She never said she had a man. She was cheating on my friend. The question was why.

A week later, I asked her on a date. She said yes. I made a reservation at a restaurant. She thought she was meeting me there, but instead her boyfriend showed up. She was caught red-handed. She couldn't lie about anything. She also couldn't keep it real with him about why she was seeing other men behind his back.

He gave her everything—I mean everything. In return, she gave him a broken heart. He was committed to someone who was not committed to him. He valued everything about her, while she valued nothing about him. She thought only about herself and her own satisfaction.

I tell people that you need to know a person before spending any type of money on that person. You don't want to look stupid at the end of the day. People are always saying they are looking for unconditional love. But you have to be careful that others don't take your kindness for weakness. You cannot let a person mistreat you and take you for granted, and yet choose to love that person regardless. Is that fair to you? What happened to the love, care, trust, and respect for yourself? You have to love without boundaries, but you also have to make sure your partner loves you the same way.

We let the love take over our minds. We don't think straight. That's why love is said to be blind. What you think you see is often an illusion. When you first meet someone, everything seems perfect—the way she talks, the way she dresses, the way she carries herself. But the only way to really know her is to follow her patterns. That's how you'll know if you're wasting time.

What sounds good in the beginning can leave you disappointed in the end. Nine times out of ten, you will go through the bullshit with bullshitters. Good talkers are often bad actors. We come across trust issues when we can't trust ourselves.

The simple fact is people get cheated on every single day. I've been cheated on before, and I've cheated too. I was immature, reckless, and hardheaded until I got my heart broken. It felt like the end of the world. It took time for my heart to recover from the pain.

Once your guard's up, it is up for a long time. No matter how nice a potential partner is to you, you will treat her like everyone else who has been trying to talk to you. If you find the right person, one who's willing to do anything for you, you'll still have the mind-set not to trust. You need to correct that. You need to understand your inner insecurities, not allow them to jeopardize your future happiness.

Trust Issues

Relationships are not complicated; people are. We all have trust issues, especially if we have been played several times. Trust is the key in any relationship. Without it, there's no relationship. It's pointless to be with someone you can't trust. If you can't build trust, don't even bother trying to start a relationship. It's not going to work out. Some people don't listen; that's why they end up hurt all the time. To avoid trust issues, keep it real from the start. Once you lie, your potential partner will think differently of you.

I've noticed people using sex to save their relationships. Honestly, sex will not save a damaged relationship. There's no point in continuing to have sex if the emotional connection is no longer there.

My best advice to everyone facing a breakup is to communicate. Make sure you show your partner that you still care. It's better to try than to give up without trying. Sex will always be there. Make sure you're still in the relationship and the feelings are mutual. Feelings go deeper than sex.

Looking for Perfection

Relationships are not perfect. If you are trying to find the perfect person, you'll be disappointed in the long run.

People expect perfection. I thought I could find the perfect person. Guess what? I didn't. I failed to realize no one in this world is perfect. We expect way too much, and at the same time, we do not to want to settle for disappointment.

Everyone has flaws. It's natural. Remember, everything can be worked on. It's all about how badly you want to work on it. The only way your relationship will last is if you and your partner keep it real with each other. If not, you're just wasting your time.

Jealousy

Jealousy can be a sign that a person deeply cares for you. I used to date a woman who got mad at me when I stared at other women. I never knew why until the day we went out to a beautiful, fancy restaurant. We were served by a waiter every woman in the place had her eyes on. The woman I was with paid attention also. She couldn't take her eyes off him. I felt the way she must have felt when I was staring at other women. I admitted to myself that I was jealous.

During the evening, I didn't act like my normal self. She noticed, so I told her. After we ate dinner and paid the tab, we took a walk in the park. I told her how I felt when she stared at another man, and she told me how she felt when I stared at other women. We communicated and agreed we needed to show respect when we were out in public with each other.

My brother once said something that makes a lot of sense: "Love looks through a telescope, while jealousy looks through a microscope." If you dwell on jealousy, you will allow yourself to be consumed by the smallest irritations in your relationship. Instead, look at the bigger picture. Use the telescope.

Friends, Friends, Friends

Friends are cool to a certain extent. You can tell them anything—*except* your relationship problems. The single ones especially will give you tips on how to keep a partner, but they can't even keep one themselves.

I think it is better never to listen to your friends. They'll always advise you to find someone better than the person you have now. Keep your personal business to yourself, no matter what. If you need to, you can figure things out with your partner. That's the point of being in a relationship.

Another place not to discuss your problems is on social media. Social media doesn't ruin relationships; what you post ruins relationships. I used to post my personal business and my relationship issues. I thought I could get help. But I was wrong. All my feedback was negative.

Some people don't care, so think twice before you post anything about your relationship. I had to learn on my own. That's why I'm giving you inside tips, so you do not make the same mistakes I've made in the past.

Rule One: Don't Rush into *Anything*

Take your time to see if this relationship is something you want. One of many reasons relationships do not last is that people rush into them. Say you've been talking to a woman for a few days, and the feeling is wonderful. She seems different from the women you've dated before. She gives you feelings of joy and excitement. You can't put your finger on it, but you love talking to her. You wonder what she is doing during the day, and you get excited when her name pops up on your phone. You find yourself smiling at text messages she's sent or even at the thought of her.

Well, duh. This is just the beginning. After a while, things start to change.

The truth is, you know nothing about this woman. What she decides to show in the beginning is not the whole person. Get to know her and learn her attitude, her personality, and her lifestyle. When you rush into something as serious as a relationship, many things are bound to happen. Love when you're ready, not when you're lonely.

The Three Cs

The three Cs are most important when in a relationship: *commitment, communication,* and *compromise.*

Most relationships fail because people don't know how to commit. Scary word? But if you love someone, why get into the relationship with the mentality of a single person? Don't hurt the one you love because you're so selfish that you can't take a risk. If the shoe were on the other foot, you wouldn't want to be hurt by the person you love. Treat her the way you want be treated.

Besides, being in a relationship with the same mentality as a single person isn't much of a challenge. If you don't commit yourself, if you don't fight the temptation to play around, the so-called relationship won't be worth the effort.

Communication. Say it with me: *com-mu-ni-ca-tion.* The biggest problem in relationships and a big reason that relationships fail is lack of communication. You must learn to talk to your partner about what's on your mind. If you can't, what's the point of being with her?

No one likes to be ignored. So when you are looking for a compatible mate, hopefully you will put that on your checklist: be a person who listens. Next, you must be able to tell your partner what you like, what you dislike, what you want to see done, and what you want to do. If you are not capable of doing this, your relationship has little to no chance of surviving.

Most people do not have the gift of mind reading. How will your partner know how you feel and be able to respect your feelings if you don't say anything? Lack of communication can be dangerous. It can lead to arguments, breaking up to make up, or breaking up to stay broken.

Lack of communication can rub a partner the wrong way. You'll find that the two of you are fighting over little things with no clear reason for it. You might say how you feel in that moment, but when things have reached the point of argument, it goes in one ear and out the other. Neither one of you has found out how to get your point across without offending the other. You've never learned how to say what's on your mind before the situation explodes.

Take a second to listen to what your partner has to say, and then respond. Not everything is going to be a fairy tale with a happy ending. Sometimes, both of you need to get something off your chests and then take time to reflect. Think about things before coming back to each other and resolving the issue.

When you learn to communicate, you can then compromise. Relationships are give and take. They are fifty-fifty, not sixty-forty or ninety-ten. It's a team effort. It takes two. Yes, you've been single and you're not used to working on a team. This is where compromise takes place. There's no such thing as being alone in a relationship. "Me" and "you" becomes "us" and "we." In relationships, you become a whole, and you have to work as a whole.

You Can't Walk Together if You Don't Agree

Many people say that social media networks are the reason some relationships fail. I'm here to tell you differently. Social media is a vehicle for your personal use. You have full control over what you write and who you write to. Do not blame a social network when your relationship fails. If you were not able to build trust with your partner before you got on the social network, how do you expect things to work when you are posting online? Of course social media is going to be the downfall of your relationship if it leads your partner to mistrust you. Everything you say and do will be held against you. Everything you say will be interpreted, and perhaps not the way you intended. Your partner will be suspicious, assumptive, and argumentative.

Not knowing each other's boundaries and the right buttons to push can also make your relationship go down the drain. No guy likes a nagging, complaining, attention-seeking woman who asks twenty-one questions. Ladies, know when to give your man space. There's no need to keep him under twenty-four-hour surveillance. I understand women love to cuddle and want to spend quality time with their men, but there is a time and place for everything. If he's going out with the fellas, let him hang with the fellas. Trust him when he says where he's going. No need to text him every five minutes, complaining and asking what he's doing, You're not his mother; know your role. Let him hang out and have a good time without having to deal with you. When he gets home, you can cuddle, ask how his day was, and spend quality time. But ladies, asking your man twenty-one questions will only drive him away.

Guys, ladies don't like a man who can't protect them, provide for them, and be there 100 percent, emotionally and physically. If your lady is there for you, money shouldn't be an issue. She'll get you on your feet and help you provide financially once you're stable. In the meantime, don't let your pride get in the way.

Relationships consist of two people: you and your partner. I understand that sometimes you need someone to talk to, but be careful who you tell your problems to, and don't tell too much. When you tell your friends every detail of your relationship, they may feel envious and start to cause problems. They may be curious. They may even try to fill your shoes. The people you bring into your relationship can quickly take the situation to an epic fail. At the end of day, it is your relationship, and you should make the decisions and solve the problems your relationship is facing. Don't let anybody else tell you what should be done.

The men in my generation think being in a relationship is about sex, money, or showing a woman off. That's a big *no*. It's about being with the person who makes you happy. Some men don't realize what a true relationship is. They're too busy getting into one simply because everyone else seems to be getting into one.

I'm not writing this book to get famous or rich. I'm writing this book to tell you *the truth*. I want my generation to understand that there's someone for everyone out there. Everyone deserves to be happy at the end of the day, even me! I know it's not an easy process, but relationships take time. Patience is the best way for everything.

That being said, relationships are not for everybody. Some people are better off being single than in a relationship. If you find yourself happy, excited, laughing, and smiling every day as a single person, why would you get into a relationship that might make that happiness disappear?

A relationship does not last when you tell people your business. We all have that issue; it's something that runs through our veins. When things are not going well, we seek the best resolution by telling everyone our problems. They likely don't care because they are busy with their own lives. You kill yourself with stress.

Some people in relationships have moved beyond being upset and angry. They're just tired—tired of putting in more effort than they'll receive. They're tired of holding on for nothing, tired of believing all of someone's lies, and tired of getting their hopes up but being disappointed again. We put our all into one person, and sometimes, that person doesn't realize how lucky she is.

My best advice for that is to let her know. After a while, that garbage gets old and played out. You get tired of trying to make things work. You get tired of giving chances. Sometimes, you need to let your partner go.

If you know someone is already taken, please respect the existing relationship. Don't be the reason why a person you respect ends up single. People don't have respect for relationships anymore. When they see a happy couple together, they wish they had something like that. Instead of being happy for the couple, they just want to ruin that happiness.

Relationships are hard; don't get me wrong. But if you love someone that much, you try *everything* to make it work—not only on your end, but on their end too. It's a two-way street.

Relationships don't get anywhere without communication. If there are no phone calls, no text messages, no emails, then how do you expect your relationship to succeed?

People say they have too many responsibilities to take time to communicate. If you can't handle your existing responsibilities, what makes you think you can take on anything else? If you can't even take care of yourself, but say you are willing to take care of someone else, that's an automatic failure. People tend to do stupid things just to end their relationships. Then they ask themselves, "Why is it that every relationship I've been in ends within a month?"

If you change some of your ways and act like yourself, then most likely the person you are trying to talk to will take you seriously. I have come across people who can't even act their age; their characters seem so plain and simple that you can figure them out in a heartbeat.

Relationships have bad times. It's up to you to decide whether the person you're with is worth working through those times. Remember, the only person you can control in a relationship is you. You cannot control what your partner is doing. No one has time to babysit or chase anyone. If you feel like you're constantly doing that, it's time to let go and wait on someone who has a better understanding.

Relationships fall apart because everyone wants to live double lives. But playing with people's emotions is negative, especially if they put their lives on hold for you. Most people don't see it like that. They think they'll never get caught. Chances are, they will. You'll end your long-term relationship for someone else who might not be as good. Just because something looks good to you doesn't mean it's good for you.

Ladies, most guys don't notice the things
you do until you stop doing them.

CHAPTER 3

Loyal Partners Are Rare

Everyone wants to be with someone who is loyal and will stay faithful in a relationship. But nowadays, loyalty is hard to find. I tell people this all the time: if you have someone who is willing to ride or die for you throughout everything, then keep them, no matter what situation you are in. Such a person is not easy to replace. You deserve to be with someone who makes you happy. You want a person who won't complicate your life, someone who won't hurt you.

Remaining loyal in a relationship shows your maturity level. Loyal men and loyal women can be found in the most unexpected places. One of your exes could hang out in the same places as you, and you'd be shocked to see her. It's funny but true. Some people don't deserve to be with a loyal partner, because they can't handle a faithful person or a real relationship.

I have my own way of defining loyalty. To me, loyalty means that your partner does not lust after other people, not even in mind. I think you would agree that this quality is pretty hard to find. You have to define for yourself what it means to be loyal. What are the things that you will tolerate in your relationship, and what won't you allow?

In this generation, it is rare to find a man or woman who will forever remain faithful to one person. Is it possible? Yes, it's possible to stay dedicated to an individual.

No one is perfect. Everyone has flaws. It's possible for a man or a woman to stay faithful, but it doesn't happen often. Each partner would have to have tremendous self-restraint and self-esteem. In this day and age, it's harder than ever to find people like this, since the media portrays being sexually promiscuous as a thing to aspire to. It's not all bad though. With society being more open about sex, people are more educated about it.

At the end of the day, you never know whether a partner is cheating on you, unless they're bad at hiding their whereabouts. Most loyal people get mistreated by partners who do not value loyalty. Often, a loyal partner gets put last on the list. They go through a lot of bullshit for no reason, period. It is not fair to them at all. But loyal people who connect with a loyal partner find themselves cherished.

It seems that nowadays people fear how they look to others. They believe staying loyal isn't a good look. They'd rather impress irrelevant people instead of the one who truly loves them. So they find themselves cheating.

Ask yourself: why the hell did you get into a relationship and waste the other person's time? Some people cheat because they feel a lack in the relationships they have, but I find that very foolish. If something is nagging you and making you feel unhappy, I suggest you sit down with your partner and talk about it. That's the best thing you can do in a relationship. Communicate with your partner so you can work through it as a team.

Loyalty Equals Royalty

People just don't understand how meaningful it is to find that one person who will ride with you till the wheels come off. The chances of that happening are very rare, and we don't always recognize it when it happens. When we come across someone who is loyal to us, chances are we mess it up, for the simple reason that we've never had someone who is willing to do everything in their power to keep us happy.

Faithful, loyal, and hardworking people of both genders do exist in this world, so don't give up hope. Relationships are often not respected because other people don't want to see you happy, no matter what. People claim to be loyal when they really are not.

I feel that men should step up to the plate more often instead of being lazy. You can't expect a woman to stay loyal if you are not doing anything to keep her, if you make her do everything on her own. That's not fair to her, especially when she's the only person who's riding with you. If you think being loyal means letting her spend her money on you, then I suggest you look up the word *loyalty* in the dictionary.

As men, we should not degrade ourselves and our self-esteem. Too often, we act as if we don't love our women, when we really do inside. On the other hand, we often bring the most money into the household and think that our women do not appreciate it, when they really do, deep down inside. Fellas, love is a beautiful thing. Don't be scared to admit it because of what people would say. Fuck what they say. Love and cherish your woman.

People break promises. Broken hearts are nothing new. We have all had relationships that we regret letting go or regret getting into. Either way, we learn from those relationships, and we know what to expect in the next. Loyal women and men need to find the values that they hold dear in another person. You may find that person in your church, in another country, anywhere. Your task is to find the one who shares your moral values. Then you have to trust that person with your heart based on what's inside her heart.

The bottom line is, don't give up on anyone you are pursuing. Take your sweet time to get to know the other person, and you will see whether she is worth your time.

Finding a Loyal Partner

As I said before, there are a lot of good people out there who are loyal, loving, outgoing, honest, considerate, and caring. You just have to pray and let God handle the rest.

People ask me sometimes how I found *the one*, and my best answer to them is, let the one find *you*. Internet dating sites could possibly help you find the one, even though I don't recommend that approach.

Nevertheless, I actually found my first true love on BlackPlanet.com. It sounds crazy but it's the truth.

No one wants to be bored or lonely all the damn time. What's fun about that? We can't tell who we are going to fall in love with. Love is unexpected for everybody out there. People need to stay true to themselves and be patient. Hopefully, the person that they've been waiting for will meet them one day. Nothing is promised in life. That's why you can't expect too much from a person who is not loyal to you.

If you use one of the dating Web sites, be careful not to come off too needy, eager to date any prospect who is friendly to you. Hold back a little while and get to know the person better before considering them your friend. Grow up a little. Stay loyal to the person you choose to spend your time with.

If you want the person to be loyal, you need to ask yourself if this relationship is what you really want for the rest of your life. Try out new things together, like bicycling, tennis, or going to a museum. Before you get into a relationship, start with a friendship. Don't rush into love. Take your time.

Loyal to a Fault

Kia's last relationship was a disaster. She caught her boyfriend cheating with her best friend. Kia is twenty years old. She is pursuing a modeling career. Her goal is to become one of the best models in the industry. She did everything in her power to keep her boyfriend happy, but like most out there, he wasn't satisfied. He knew she was a good woman who didn't deserve to be treated the way he was treating her. She knew her worth and left him.

Kia told me that among today's youth, loyalty is just a word with little meaning. She wanted every single woman around the world to hear what she said.

"I think the real problem is that people do not understand the term. Most people say they are looking for someone who is loyal, but when they get that, it's like it doesn't even matter.

"Relationship after relationship, I showed loyalty, and was left with nothing but a broken heart. Despite the fact that all my relationships ended badly, I remained the same. But I did begin to question myself. I wondered if I was too loyal. I just didn't get it.

"In the dictionary, *loyalty* is defined as devotion and faithfulness to one or more objects. And I was nothing but loyal. I was focused on the person I was in a relationship with. No one mattered besides him. I showed him my devotion by being there for him when things were going well, and I was there ten times as much when things were horrible. Through the arguments and breakups, I managed to swallow my pride.

"I put things aside and gave him a support system when he was in the hospital, undergoing surgery. We weren't together at the time. I knew he was talking to another woman, but I felt that it was my job to be there for him when nobody else was—even the woman he was dealing with. My friends told me I was an idiot for making that trip to the hospital. I agreed, but I needed to be there for him, to show him that not all women are the same and that I actually cared for him.

"Every time the doctor came to check up on him, I was asked if I was his significant other. Deep down I wanted to scream yes, but my mouth said, 'No, I am not. I'm just a friend here to show support.' The open wounds he had caused were reopened. It killed me inside to know that everything I had done for the past year meant little or nothing. The loyalty I showed him meant nothing. It sucks when you put your all into something or someone and you do not get the same thing in return. Instead, your good, loyal heart is torn down and sealed behind a brick wall for the next guy to try to tear down.

"Many people fail to realize what they have until it becomes what they *had*, and by that time, it's too late. Not only is it too late for you to get that person back, but it is harder for that person to remain loyal to their next partner. The lack of loyalty is why relationships don't last or are messed up. When a good person has been hurt time and time again, it's hard to be strong, shake things off, and pretend that things are okay when everything is falling apart. It is hard not to mix up the past with the present.

"Just like positive experiences, the negative ones are learning experiences. I learned not to change even when those around me changed. I learned how to weed out the real from the fake, when to fall back, when to play my part and let others play theirs, how to react to certain situations, and how to communicate about my feelings. But the number one thing I learned was not to waste time on someone who wasn't giving me the same things I was giving him."

Kia is now single and focusing on her career. She is probably talking to a couple of people, the kind of people she can see herself being with in the future. I'm happy that she took the right step to move on with her life.

It's perfectly fine if you feel hurt, neglected, and rejected. Without any of the pain, how do you enjoy the happiness you are longing for? How do you know how to deal with someone else's situation if you haven't gone through anything yourself? You don't! Stay positive. Remain true to yourself, because in the end that's all you have.

You turn on the news, and you hear things about global warming and saving the polar bears from extinction. Well, it's the same thing with loyal guys. Loyal guys will most likely go extinct along with the polar bears. Women can't save them because many women do not know how to tell the difference between a good guy and a bad one. The reason for that is simple. Bad guys always know the right things to say to get what they want. Likewise, the good guys always fall for the bad women who portray themselves as someone they're not. It's hard to tell who is loyal and who is only out for your goods. Good guys usually finish last.

Finding a Loyal Partner

Sometimes you've got to let people go so they can be who they are. There's not enough loyalty and unconditional love anymore because people are looking in the wrong places. Sometimes, I feel that my best friends and I are the only loyal people we know.

My friend Peter, who is twenty-six years old, lives in New York City. He is not in school at the moment because of financial issues. He has been loyal to his women, and he has always been cheated on. I think he falls for the bad apples. I constantly tell him to look somewhere new instead of in the same old places.

At the same time, tons of women ask me if there are any decent, loyal men. Yes, there are plenty out there. But in today's society, women always get screwed over. I'm sure every woman could say that about herself.

It's very hard on the men's side too. We don't know if a woman is going to turn out to be a gold digger or a reformed slut looking for a decent man to pay for her and a baby. With no-fault divorce, men don't know if we're going to get traded in for a bigger meal ticket. We are very cautious.

I use to pride myself on treating women well and with respect. But now I'm in my twenties, I've been with one too many women who thought it was their right to be in the friend zone with a smart, decent, loyal guy in his twenties. They wanted no strings attached. They thought they could have fun with anyone, then reach out to the good guy in the friend zone when they reached their thirties, after they'd had their fun and were ready for a meal ticket and kids.

Most decent guys are defensive to protect themselves. You've got to give a little to get something. A lot of people have wonderful relationships, and many are now *not* single. I think that men's idea of loyalty is very different from women's idea. Most of my friends go into their twenties and thirties still deciding if they want to settle down or continue to look for their soul mates.

Women and men that don't cheat are usually happy with their partners and have been with them for years. There are predatory women out there who will try to entice men, so it's up to us men to decide not to cheat.

Loyal men don't want the drama. They have values, and respect and love their partners too much. Why risk it all for a fling or one-night stand? Once trust is broken, it takes years to regain. Just because someone looks good doesn't mean they are good for you.

I have a close friend who is so in love with his girlfriend, that is all he talks about. When he's with her, he doesn't look at other women. When he goes somewhere and women try to hit on him, he ignores them. The idea of cheating makes him sick to his stomach. He thinks he is lucky to have the perfect woman in his life.

I wish more men were like my friend. He dedicates his time and energy to this relationship. I am proud and happy that he has found love with the right woman. She appreciates and accepts him for who he is. That's what I call loyalty—sticking with each other through thick and thin and not letting anything come between you.

Some men and women are single to this day because they've been hurt too many times and see potential partners as just like partners from their past. I am so sorry for them. But not all women and men are like this. I'm sorry for those who never got the chance to have a happy, fulfilling relationship. But you still can.

If we knew the full truth about the people in our lives, I think we'd be shocked. A man might choose to be fully committed to a relationship, but he will likely see it as a sacrifice. It will be hard for him. I've never met a man who has not done something that would constitute cheating—or at least who would have been willing to do that.

But I also believe a strong, independent, loyal woman won't let any man get the best of her. A woman of strength should give herself the best, no matter how hard the road ahead is. Women should keep faith, and find the strength to overcome any obstacle that comes her way. A woman who is a strong leader is respectful to everyone. That doesn't mean she has to tolerate men's bad behavior and disrespect.

The negative experience that loyal women have gone through can make them doubt relationships. Even the nicest of men have been known to stray. Men who love their partners with all their hearts, who have the most beautiful partners—all types of men do dirt behind their partners' backs, deceive them, and break their hearts.

All for what, people? A one-night stand or a sleazy affair that might not even last a month? People confuse love with lust. It makes a lot of us wonder what we have to do to stop our partners from going elsewhere. Are we doing something wrong? Can we prevent it? Or are men and women incapable of being satisfied with what they already have?

I agree completely with that saying, "It is better to have loved and lost then never to have loved at all." Losing someone you love can make you stronger every day and more determined to get what you want the next time around.

If I act on love and lose, I will be more cautious in the future. At times, this can be a bad thing. The majority of the time, it helps me distinguish the good women from the bad. Sometimes I think I recognize them a little too late, but at least I do recognize them.

I have witnessed many unfaithful men and women. I have seen it in the past, I am seeing it in the present, and I expect it will continue in the future. We all ask questions, and we want answers that give us faith that love still exists, that there is someone out there who is willing to make us happy.

If your time hasn't come yet, wait your turn. Everything will fall into place. If it doesn't happen down the road, it wasn't meant to be. If you believe in love and God, you should continue. Don't let anyone change your mind. Continue to be that loving, caring, sweet, honest person. Never change for anybody who won't change for themselves. Be yourself. If they don't like you, then you don't need them in your life.

Defining Loyalty for Yourself

Each person has his or her own definition of loyalty. If you define loyalty by saying that your significant other cannot ever lust after another person, even in mind, then that is pretty difficult to find. If you define loyal to mean that your partner may not have an emotional or sexual connection to another while in a relationship with you, then you can probably find a partner who fits that definition. If loyalty is important to you, articulate what it means to you to be loyal (things you will tolerate and things you won't).

As an example, I have heard it said that kissing another on the lips while in a relationship does not constitute cheating. I disagree completely. People who think that way are the ones doing all the cheating. It's very sad to see them waste other people's time in relationships. I guess everybody wants to get into a relationship and act like it's cool to have the freedom of a single man while enjoying the commitment from a partner. It's crazy how people will let you down in one way or another. Some of us would rather not love at all, because we don't trust potential partners. We can blame society for these problems.

I feel sorry for women. It's very hard on them, because most men don't want a relationship. They just want ass all the damn time. Some women don't mind if their men are poor or rich; they just want one man to prove that all men are not the same. Remember to be friends first. Women are tired of going out of their way for someone who doesn't do anything in return.

Be happy to have a woman who's there for you 24/7 and who is willing to make time for you. The world is changing, which means the people who live in it are changing. If you don't believe in love or relationships, stay single for the rest of your life. Let everyone else enjoy the happiness that they work so hard to get.

People, listen to me. There are such things as loyal people, even though they are truly hard to find. They won't be perfect, but they will be there when you need someone.

Loyal people don't cheat. They don't have the time for that. They're too busy trying to make someone else happy. Someone who will put your happiness before theirs is someone who truly loves you. Relationships like that don't come around often, but you can find one. I am happy to say I'm with a woman who I know would never hurt me in any way.

Sometimes you need to step back and stop painting everyone with the same brush. You can't judge a book by its cover; you have got to open the book first. That's where you will find that not every man or woman is the same.

The best way not to get caught
cheating is not to cheat at all.

CHAPTER 4

Why Do Women and Men Cheat in Their Relationships?

Women and men have a history of cheating that goes way back. Men and women are different, and everyone has their own reason why they cheat. Women cheat off their emotions, and guys cheat off of temptations. Only the cheater knows exactly why he or she cheats. The reasons include unhappiness, depression, frustration, and sadness. Some want that one-night stand, and some want to have their cake and eat it too. Meanwhile, the person who has been dealing everything straight looks like a damn fool. It's a sad case but it's also the truth.

No one person can give you everything. That does not mean you have the right to go out there and get it from someone else. What's the point of being in a committed relationship if all your partner does is cheat and mistreat you? People think cheating is the right thing to do, when it's totally the opposite. Cheating destroys everything that you and your partner have built. It takes away your happiness. It makes you weak, miserable, unwanted, and depressed. It turns your whole world upside down.

Everyone has a reason to cheat. Instead, they could've just broken off their relationship and moved on. Sometimes people don't think. They take action without considering their partner's feelings. But if a

person really loves you and the relationship you are in together, that person won't ruin it for a one-night stand.

Cheating is a choice, not a mistake. Cheaters will of course tell you what they did was an accident. But how could it be an accident? It takes two to mingle.

You deserve to be with someone who makes you happy, someone puts a smile on your face, and someone who won't hurt you. People will continue to treat you like shit if you allow them to.

Some people are never satisfied. You can give them the world, and they'll still find a way to cheat on you. You will ask yourself why. "What have I done wrong to deserve this treatment?"

Pause. Never, ever blame yourself. You have done your best. If your partner can't see that, it is time to move on and save yourself the heartbreak. Seriously, the worst feeling in the world is knowing you did your best and discovering it still wasn't good enough.

If you are giving more then you should, that's not a good relationship. I advise you to leave and wait for someone who is going to appreciate you for you. Don't get upset or frustrated; let your ex-partner be. Don't waste your time on revenge. Those who hurt you will eventually face their own karma. Women and men should know cheating and sneaking around gets old after a while. Everyone should want a reach a point where they're mature enough to stay faithful to one partner and want something real.

More men need to learn how to treat women with respect, and more women need to understand that all men are not the same. Men, make sure you use the time that she gives you to make things right. Time is everything. Every minute counts if you have serious intentions. Your first words should never be, "When you coming to my crib to chill?" She knows you want sex. Why bring her to an environment where she isn't going to be comfortable? Take her out on a date to show that you respect her. Stop and think. When you approach her, give her and her body respect.

Women, every single man out there is not the same as the guy who hurt you. There are a lot of decent men in this world. You cannot see that if you are busy cheating on the good ones. If you cannot see yourself with a man forever, let him be. Break up with him instead of cheating; that's the best way to end things.

The problem with my generation is that people lead others on, confusing them. A person who approaches you never tells you how it is from the beginning. Sometimes partners love each other, but can't be together because the loyalty and understanding are not there. Be warned if you feel that someone else understands you more than your partner does. It means your partner is not there to listen to you—or that you don't trust your partner enough to be honest.

Besties

My generation has this thing we call *bestie*. It's a slang word for *best friend*. We all know women who have male best friends and men who have female best friends. In my opinion, feelings always get involved when women and men cross that best-friend boundary.

I've learned this on my own. I used to have a female best friend. She was always there for me when I needed someone to talk to about my relationship and my problems. She would tell me to work it out with the person I was with. No matter what was going on, my bestie was there for me. I had a gut feeling that she liked me but never told me. I had to respect her for that, because she respected that I was in a relationship.

As the days passed by, I started to like her and catch the feeling. She was always there when I was having issues. My partner was not listening to anything I said. She wasn't trying to make things better.

Finally, I started taking things seriously with my best friend. We talked, laughed, play-fought, and kissed. I knew then we were more than best friends. Feelings had gotten involved. I dumped the woman I'd been with and started going out with my best friend.

Everything between us was perfect until a few weeks later. I knew if I broke up with her, the things we'd gone through would be wasted— the time shared, the phone conversations, the dates, just everything. But I wasn't feeling it like I thought I should be.

So I ended it. I broke her heart for no reason. Because I was confused and didn't know what I wanted anymore, I ended up losing my best friend.

Everyone out there, if you have a best friend, just keep things the way they are now. If you take that next step, there is no turning back. Everything will be different, no matter how hard you try to fix things. I've learned from experience, so I am sharing this with the world.

When your partner starts acting funny toward you, it is one of two things: either they are currently cheating on you, or they have been cheating on you. That's why most people don't allow that opposite-sex bestie bullshit in their relationship. They know if anything happens in the relationship, their partner is going to run to that best friend.

I believe two people who are in a relationship together should work it out together. Friends tend to put thoughts into your head. Some make you feel you should go out and cheat instead of working on your issues. It goes both for men and women.

No one can control your relationship. At the end of the day, it's up to you if you want to tell your "best friend" your entire business. People end up sleeping with their best friends because they've been hurt and there's no one else around to lean on. If your partner is giving her male best friend more attention then you, there's something wrong going on. You have a right to find out. Don't sit around and act like nothing is going on. When your feelings are telling you that something isn't right, listen to them. You can't complain about getting cheated when you had an opportunity to solve the issue.

We all live and learn. We expect our partners to do the same. If you and your partner can't see eye to eye, make sure to end your relationship on a good note. Always forgive but never forget.

A Strong Relationship Is More than Sex

Women say that even if there is no chance their partner will find out, less than 2 percent are likely to cheat. But 5 percent of women admit to having cheated on their current relationships.

Men say more than 5 percent are very likely to cheat if there's no chance their partner will find out. Yet less than 3 percent of men have cheated on their current partner.

Additionally, 46 percent of men said that the appeal of cheating on their partners is that a mistress might do things in the bedroom that men wouldn't dare ask their girlfriends or wives to do. Women don't like having sex all the time, so I really understand where these men are coming from. If you're thinking about cheating because your needs are not met, speak to your partner and let her know. Remember, relationships are about learning and growing with each other.

When you enter a relationship, don't expect everything to be perfect, because it never is. Cheating is the last thing you should be thinking about. If you and your partner create new tricks in the bedroom, you'll notice the difference the down the line. But if you see your partner is not willing to have sex with you the way she used to, either the sex got boring or she doesn't like having sex with you anymore.

Every woman is different; every man is different. Everybody's relationships are different. So I suggest you find a partner who makes you smile, who checks up on you often to see if you're okay, who watches out for you, who wants the best for you, who cries and pleads for you, who sacrifices every little thing for you, who loves you unconditionally, who respects you, who never gets tired of forgiving you, and who is always available for you. Don't let that person go. Keep a partner like that close to your heart, and don't take her for granted.

People like that are hard to find. You may not value what your partner does for you, but someone out there admires what she does for you. She may replace you one day.

We all need someone who is prepared to answer a million questions, laugh a lot, respect our families, laugh at our musical outbursts and random dancing, hang out with our friends, talk to us when we're sad, shed tears of joy, get into those deep talks about life, explore our imaginations with us, help our dreams come true, walk in the rain holding our hands, send us random texts throughout the day, make useless arguments, and accept us for who we are. Some people forget all the things that matter the most in a partner. Value a partner's feelings at all times. You do not know how much courage it took for your partner to tell you how she really feels about you.

Cheating for Revenge

Suppose you found out your girlfriend was being unfaithful to you. Maybe you feel that the only you can relieve your stress and anger is by doing the same thing. For many people, the only way to get back at their cheating partner is to even the score. Some people, in other words, cheat back.

In general, women are quick to forgive men for unfaithful behavior. Maybe women fear being alone forever, or that the right guy will never come. Some women might even blame themselves for not having sex often enough. They may take steps to improve their relationships. Some women let their men get away with murder right before their eyes. They may have lost feelings for the men they used to love because the cheating and lying have been going for many years. But they stay because the relationship remains part of them—separating seems too painful.

In the end, cheating is no joking matter. If your partner is cheating, it may be because your partner is not happy in the relationship or has issues to address. Cheating might feel good as a quick escape from a problem, but in reality, the problem will always remain there.

The Warning Signs of Cheating

Women badly want to know why men cheat, and I'll tell you why. Cheating happens when a woman starts pulling away. Men will then become more distant and spend less time with their partner. Noticing the signs early on can save a lot of heartaches, believe me.

Here are the warning signs:

- His patterns are not the same anymore.
- He doesn't buy you flowers like he used to.
- He stops taking you out.
- He picks up your calls and says he'll call you back, but he never does.

These are a few of the many things you are likely to notice when your man is cheating on you.

Stupid and selfish, some men think the grass is greener on the other side of the fence. Men lack self-control. Whether a man gets caught or not, he'll still lose out. He'll lose his self-respect.

All men, at some level, know that cheating is wrong. Otherwise why would they be hiding it? If he is keeping you as secret, chances are you're not the only one. If he never introduces you to his family or friends, you're a walking fool. It's not your fault, so don't blame yourself at all. Men cheat because they think women don't know.

As economic conditions improve for women, the concern about cheating men will become less important. Note also, even today, how fast women who are not poor will change men, but don't necessarily dump those who cheat.

Men cheat because women are ignorant, weak, and easily persuaded to be doormats. If a woman refuses sex with a selfish, power-hungry, and oversexed male, it only makes him want her more. If women were smart, they would never have sex.

Tips for Cheating Men

Men, stop pursuing sex with strangers. Try to keep one woman saying yes. This is the real challenge for you. If more men followed this advice, they could probably find the women they want. Instead, men are busy sleeping with every woman out there, thinking they will be happy at the end of the day.

Ladies, whether a man cheats is up to him. The temptation can be greater or less depending on circumstances, but ultimately it's his choice. No man should blame any woman. It takes two to cheat, and if one is married, he is going to take the fall. If both are married, they both are probably going to fall. If you cheat and lie and do it enough, you're going to get caught. Men cheat because they can; women cheat because they can.

Women Who Cheat

A lot of men want to know why women cheat. The reasons vary, but "it was a mistake" is never the real reason.

Some women suffer from low self-esteem due to insecurities in their relationships. This feeling can cause them to seek attention from someone different. There's always that one guy who compliments her, gives her the attention she wants, and is willing to fulfill her needs. This boosts her self-esteem and makes her feel good. A guy on the side makes her feel comfortable lets her forget her insecurities for a little while.

Many times, temptation can overpower any reluctance to commit infidelity. It's always a struggle, but in the very present moment, everything wrong can feel so right.

There are women who just like the thrill. They seek the excitement of sneaking off with someone else and experiencing something new. Some women have problems talking about everything that's not going right in their sex lives. It's hard to bring up things you want to try or how you would like to be pleased without offending a man. A woman may have wondered how it would feel to have someone she's seen in the grocery store get between her legs. When an opportunity presents itself, these women don't hesitate because of the excitement and the curiosity that's been there for so long.

When a man fails to give his partner the attention and affection she desires, she will seek it in other places. Women don't seek in other places on purpose. But when she finds herself alone for many nights because her man is at the office late and comes home tired, not paying her any mind, she starts to want some company. Maybe she goes looking for a friend to listen to her problems. Everybody knows the only thing women ask for is someone to listen to them. They look for someone to comfort them. If she finds a guy who is her "friend," who is there for her, who listens and shows that he cares and is interested, then feelings begin to grow. One thing leads to another. By the time sex happens, it's too late to apologize.

Revenge is another reason for a woman to cheat. They always say two wrongs don't make a right, but in this case the woman thinks the old saying doesn't apply. A suspicious woman will always think that her man is cheating on her. Why? If her suspicion is based on evidence of probable cause, nine times out of ten, she's right—she's being cheated on. A woman's intuition is rarely wrong.

Then the thinking goes, if you can't beat him, join him. There's no better way to give him a taste of his own medicine than having an affair. Maybe she'll choose that guy who's been asking her out and she's been rejecting because she was committed. Maybe she'll choose one of his homeboys. Women are spiteful. Once you hurt them, all they want is for you to feel the same way they've felt.

If her suspicion is in the back of her head with no evidence, a woman's natural instinct is to cheat before her man gets to do it. It makes her feel like she has the upper hand. She can't get hurt because she's jumped the gun before her man had the chance.

When women have suspicion without proof, it's caused by insecurities, he-said she-said, or past relationships. As a man, you will never understand the complexity of how women think. Regardless, insecurities, not being given enough attention, excitement, or revenge never justify cheating.

It's Not Cheating if You Don't Commit

There can be no cheating unless there was a commitment in the first place. If anyone, man or woman, wants more than one partner, the rules are simple: don't get married, and don't demand exclusivity from your partners. Make your intentions clear up front. No one cares anymore if people don't get married or don't have a lifetime partner. But a person who makes a commitment or takes a vow should honor it. Everyone gets tempted. That doesn't mean one has to give in to temptation.

It's sad when a woman is willing to do everything to be with her man, and he does everything to be with the next woman.

CHAPTER 5

Speaking to the Ladies

Every single woman who's reading this chapter right now: I appreciate you, and you are truly beautiful. I mean that from the bottom of my heart. Women are the best gift from God. They're sweet, spiritual, valuable, beautiful, smart, intelligent, caring, and strong. I respect women because without my mother, I wouldn't be here.

Special thanks to all the single mothers and to all the strong, independent women who don't take shit from any man. I realized throughout my years of dating women that women don't really ask for much. They want the simplest things. Most men don't know that because they are too busy not paying attention.

Pussy Rules

Every woman has a weak point. Even the strongest ones need kisses and hugs to convince her that you care. Men's biggest downfall is pussy. What man would resist pussy that is thrown at him? Women use that as their biggest advantage to get what they want from men. Men are too blind to see that, but they fall for it instantly. Women know men will do anything for pussy. A man will throw dirt on his own best friend to get what he wants.

New pussy is good, but fellas, you need to understand the good women out here. You can sleep with one million women and think you're that dude—until you get sent up to prison, beaten down, or sent to your death bed, and that one woman, the woman you abused, beat up, disrespected, cheated on, lied to, hurt, and embarrassed, comes through for you.

She looks out for you every time your broke ass needs money. She is always there when you have court. She never stands you up once. She always holds you down like a real woman should. She's never left your side. If that's not loyalty, I don't know what is.

This is something I will never understand about some guys. They want to talk to a whole bunch of women, but they get mad when their partners talk to other dudes. You can't get mad at her if she's doing the same thing that you're doing! Don't expect her to feel no type of way, especially if you're doing that shit right in front her face like she doesn't know.

Women Know Everything!

I've learned a couple of things about women. One of those things is that they know *everything*. Most of them just don't say anything. That's how a lot of men get caught up in their own lies—they think she doesn't know. Trust me, she knows. The truth shall set you free. I'm tired of seeing all these good women get hurt by lame dudes who aren't worth it.

Ladies, open up your eyes. Men stick around in the short term to get what they want out of you. Then they'll toss you over the side like you're trash. Stop going hard for guys who don't do the same for you. I'm tired of seeing women cry and complain over these low-class men. Y'all are so caught up in teenage puppy love, you forget who you are.

If he makes you mad more than he makes you happy, leave him.

If you find yourself broke all the time because you are looking out for him, leave him.

Sometimes, ladies, you need to put yourselves first. You are not making a selfish decision. You are just learning from your previous mistakes. No man has control over you, so don't be dumb. Don't let a man overpower you. No one can take your worth away from you. Some men just don't get it until you leave their asses behind.

Like, dude, you had a good woman in your life. You cheated on her, stole from her, and neglected her. And you wonder why she left your sorry ass? Why she doesn't text you or call you anymore? And when she does text you, she never says those sweet things that used to put a smile on your face. She takes her sweet time texting you one-word responses. When you try to start an argument with her, you can tell she doesn't give two shits anymore. She makes you think twice before opening your mouth. You have a feeling that she's sleeping with someone else. Guys call her and text her right in front of your face, and she actually answers. You can see she's moving on with her life, talking to other guys and going on dates.

Now your dumb ass starts to realize how beautiful she really is. *Now* she's an amazing woman, isn't she? Well, too bad, because you *lost* her, you idiot.

There was a time when you were her world, her pride and joy, her everything. She really wanted you. You pushed her aside for hoes. You failed to realize that, unlike the rest, she wasn't afraid to walk away. She was strong enough to let go. Now, all of a sudden, you love her! After all the damage you've done. Do you even know how much pain you caused her? It's a ton. So don't come around with your "I miss you" bullshit, because she's already gone.

Measuring Your Self-Worth

1. Some women don't realize their worth. They're too busy trying to be the perfect woman for the perfect man who doesn't exist in this world. Ladies, value yourself first. If you don't, who will?

Self-worth doesn't come from what you do. Self-worth comes from who are you and loving yourself. Learn how to love yourself by taking the small steps I have listed below.

- Don't skip your physical. Make doctor appointments when they are needed.
- Make other important appointments and be sure you keep them.

- Stay focused on your tasks.
- Do things you enjoy, like yoga, movies, dinner with friends, dancing, and meeting new people.
- Learn to open your heart to those who love you.
- Let God into your life.
- Watch other people love you; it will make you love yourself even more.
- Pray to God to make you a better person.
- Never pretend to love yourself, because you will end up hurting yourself.
- Read books you can relate to.
- Stop trying to control everything in your world, including guys.
- If you have children, spend time with them instead of chasing guys.
- Spend time with a boyfriend or husband who loves you.
- Stop being everyone's savior.
- Stop trying to be perfect.
- Stop listening to other people and start listening yourself.
- Stay positive all day.
- You don't need him if he is always hurting you and putting you down.
- Never stop loving yourself for him.
- Stop putting yourself last on the list.
- Ask yourself: if he really loves you, why isn't he there with you?
- Never settle for what you do not deserve.
- Watch who you bring into your life.
- Learn how not to give a fuck at times.
- Be strong and independent; don't depend on any man.
- Stop letting people use you and your hard-earned money.
- Don't set up yourself for failure.

These steps will not only make you feel good, they will give you strength to become a better woman. Once you value your worth, you will never settle for anything less.

I hate to see a real woman go to waste because of the time she threw away on a man who didn't appreciate her. Women are queens, and they should be treated as such. Well, the good women, at least.

Actions Speak Louder than Words

I know why some women put up with the shit that they do: because the love is so strong, it's hard to let go. Right, ladies? But that doesn't mean you should stay around and find yourself crying every single night, worrying about who he's with. Why should you go through that stress? You're just trying be a good woman to your man. His selfish ass doesn't see that.

Ladies, I'm not telling you not to be there for him. Every woman should take care of her man. But no woman should have to raise a grown man either. Tell him to get a job. Don't let him depend on your income. He'll make a habit of it. You are not his mother, so why are you pampering him? What the hell is he bringing to the table every day? What bills is he paying? What is he doing with his life, period?

It's not fair to you that you have to get up every single morning while he sleeps all day. To make matters worse, you pay for his cell phone while he flirts and talks with other women. He doesn't have time to search for a job, but he has time to talk to women all day.

If you don't change anything soon, you'll be hurt in the long run. Trust and believe me. He apologizes when he has done something wrong, but how many times are you going to accept his apologies? Apologies don't fix a broken heart.

Accepting this behavior makes you weak, makes you look at guys differently. It takes away everything that you think a relationship should be. It makes you give up on hope and love, something I hate seeing women go through.

A guy who's worth your time is one who won't dip on you when you are having problems. He won't go to a better-looking woman. He doesn't want you just for material and physical things. He loves you and respects you and your decisions. He won't take you away from your friends and family. He's not afraid to show you off and be with you in public. He talks to you with the same respect in person and when texting. He loves you unconditionally.

Ladies, if he is just telling and not showing you, he is not a man of his word. At the end of the day, actions speak louder than words.

Guys must think women are mind readers, because sometimes they barely talk to women. How do you expect her to keep feeling you if you go days without talking to her? How do you expect her to take things seriously? If you're replying slowly every time she texts you, if you keep going MIA on her, how do you expect her to not get bored with you?

Most guys say they want a "good woman," but when they meet one, they treat her like dirt and chase after hoes. A woman who stays with you after you cheated on her, sticks with you when you don't have a dollar to your name, and has your back when everyone else has given up on you—that woman *deserves the world and everything in it*. If you can't give it to her, let her go. She should be happy, even if it's not with you. And don't be upset when the next man takes her and appreciates what you didn't.

I don't understand men anymore. It's like they don't want a classy woman who doesn't give it up the first night and has a bright future. Instead, they want the other type of women, the ones who give it to them easy, no questions asked. It's not all sad, but it makes good women look bad.

Single Mothers

You know another thing I find very sad? Women having babies with guys who can't even take care of themselves. Ladies, please, listen to me. Stop having kids with guys who are not going to be there for you. Teach your son what a real man is supposed to be.

There are women who don't listen and end up paying the price. They find themselves taking care of their babies alone. Being a single mother is tough. It's stressful. I respect all the single mothers who manage to hold it down regardless, no matter what. If they have to work two jobs, day and night, to support their families, they will. That is what is keeping food in their children's mouths.

I know a single mother who raised four kids alone. She knew not to introduce them to different men every year. If she had, her kids would've thought she was a hoe. She stuck to herself and didn't ask anyone for help. If she had, they would've throw it right in her face. I respect her till this day; she's a real woman who deserves a real man.

I hate it when women have their children around multiple men, dying for someone to play stepdad to them. Nine times out of ten it doesn't work out. Something always messes things up.

Before a man respects you, ladies, you need to respect yourselves. The way you act toward a man at the beginning sets the tone. Once a man sees how you act toward him, he will act the same way toward you. A real woman keeps herself classy and her house clean and well organized. The laundry basket is emptied every other weekend. She's well-dressed when she's attending a meeting. Her hair is on point. She never swears. She behaves gracefully in all situations. She has more than enough patience to take care of her family. She has a smile on her lips and a kind word for everyone.

Some women have a bad habit of comparing themselves to other women. I find that ridiculous. There's always someone with a better smile, nicer clothes, skinnier waist, brighter eyes, and more amazing hair. Don't put yourself down. You can be happy with the way you look. The number one thing is to be yourself.

A woman gets jealous because she's afraid of losing the man she loves. When she sees you talking to a lot of women, she gets upset and nervous. When she's not around you and she hears about you seeing another woman, she starts to assume things. Her heart drops.

Ladies, I know you want that happiness: waking up in the middle of the night, shifting under the blankets, and feeling the heart of the person you love. You see him in his most peaceful and innocent moments. He breathes as though the weight of the world lies on anyone's shoulder but his own. You smile and kiss his face in the gentlest manner so as not to wake them. You know it doesn't get any better.

No man should cheat on you or treat you badly, regardless of the situation.

You Get What You Put In

Some guys feel they can play with women's hearts, but when it's all said and done, dudes will be the ones with the broken hearts. Don't hurt the one you love, because in the end you will regret it. Don't expect a woman to be faithful when you are cheating. Don't expect a woman to have a whole bunch of good qualities when you don't. Don't expect a woman not to flirt on social media when you are. Basically what I'm saying to every guy out there is you get what you put in. It should be a two-way street, not a one-way.

Ladies, I know you might feel shy around your man. But if you feel comfortable around him, you can act silly. You can sing and play-fight with him. You can be weird, dance, scream, joke, laugh, and cry with him. Be yourself. There's nothing like a woman who's comfortable around her own man. Show him your true colors so he can do the same. Things like this always take time. They don't happen overnight.

Women want that special man in their lives who isn't afraid to do things for them. If you need anything from the store, like tampons, he'll get them for you. He'll go to Victoria's Secret and help you pick out cute bras and panties. He'll help you paint your nails and toes and do your makeup before the two of you hit the bar. He'll help you with your hair before you go to work or school. This type of guy will do anything to see you smile. That's the man you want in your life. He knows at the end of the day that you deserve it all.

But too often women reject men like that. When you want him, he doesn't want you. When he wants you, you don't want him. When you both want each other, something messes it up, like it wasn't meant for you to be with him.

Ladies, love doesn't hate you, abuse you, cheat on you, do you wrong, or make you miserable and frustrated at the same time. It doesn't abandon you, beat on you, and talk down to you. Those are the actions of people who don't love you. Your partner may leave you for another woman because he thinks the grass is greener on the other side. But everything on the other side doesn't seem so sweet after a while. He'll realize he made a big mistake. It will only take a few weeks before he shows up on your doorstep again, this time with flowers.

But don't be a fool. There are only two possible reasons for him to come back: the woman he was with didn't put up with the nonsense that you did, or he just got tired of everything that she was putting him through.

This is your chance to reject him and make it clear you are no longer interested in his childish ways. Tell him to go find someone who can deal with his bullshit. Make sure you speak your mind. Don't hold back; tell him how you feel. Tell him everything, because once you do, you'll feel relief.

Why would you want to take back a man who left you for no reason? He basically thought he could live life like a celebrity. He thought wrong.

Some men will never learn till you banish them from your life. There's plenty of other good men out there dying to replace him, so why stress yourself? Make sure you get up every morning, go to the bathroom, and look at yourself in the mirror. You are *beautiful, smart,* and *independent.* If he doesn't see that, then trust me—the next man will. There is nothing wrong with you. I tell you honestly: there's something wrong with him.

A real man is someone who is capable of remaining faithful, loyal, committed, and honest. If he doesn't do these things, he is not a real man. You are just wasting your time, period.

Genetics

Why do women act the way they do?

One of my lady friends is studying at John Jay College of Criminal Justice. Jessica Cruz is twenty-four years old. She's also single, after catching her boyfriend sleeping with one of the sisters. Ever since, she has kept to herself and never gotten into another relationship. She answered my question this way.

"Hmmm … I would say it's genetics. Women are all the same in a sense. We are emotional creatures. We are natural nurturers and caregivers. We are taught to be ladies, although not all girls follow this path. From childhood to early teens, women are taught how to be Susie Homemakers. Playing house and using Easy-Bake Ovens prepare us to be women. We are the way we are because it isn't something easy for us to escape."

The female chromosome is made the same as the male chromosome but the clusters are different. The female chromosome works on her hormones, blood pressure, and heart.

I asked another lady friend about her last relationship. She said, "It's so hard to love when you can't distinguish what's real from what's fake, when you can't trust anyone because you've been hurt so many times, or when your insecurities somehow get the best of you. All of my past relationships have put me in a position where it's hard to trust anybody, especially when it comes to a potential partner.

"How do you know that he's not whispering sweet nothings just to get your goods? How can I trust that he knows his boundaries when I'm not around? I've given my all and remained loyal. Time after time, relationship after relationship, I am left with *nothing*. Each relationship has the same ending, which causes me to believe that all guys are the same. All they want is have sexual intercourse and leave a woman picking up every piece of her heart that they have broken.

"It didn't add up. I have played my role. I've tried to keep them happy. But they always seemed to look for more, never satisfied with the girl who had so much to offer and was willing to give them the world.

"After a while, I decided to sit back, reevaluate the past, and ask myself, 'Was it me? Was it something I was doing or not doing?' Yes, the past has left me with deep scars. It has built a wall so thick and tall that it is nearly impossible to break down. But it has also taught me what I don't want in a relationship and what I was not going to settle for. It has taught me to love myself so I can love someone else, to accept my flaws so I no longer feel so insecure. Being insecure and having trust issues has caused me to be bipolar in my relationships without meaning to be.

"All I need is someone willing to take the time to sit down and listen to the things that I've been through so they can get a better understanding of why I act and react the way I do. I want someone to be genuine and real so there's no mixed signals. I want someone to reassure me that everything will be all right, that I've made the right decisions about committing.

"All I've ever asked for was time, but I guess that was asking for too much."

Every woman has gotten hurt, but it doesn't mean they have given up. It made my friend a stronger person.

Ladies, one last thing: don't ever say you're not good for him. If he can't see how amazing and beautiful you are, then he is the one who's not good enough. Always remember that.

The person you love the most
can hurt you the most.

CHAPTER 6

Temporary Feelings and How to Get Out of an Unhealthy Relationship

We often find ourselves breaking up with our loved ones after all the ups and downs we've been through. There is such a buildup of pain that you want to move on with your life, but it's hard because of all the memories you shared and all the things you promised each other.

Maybe you decided to talk to other people so you could get your mind off your former partner, but deep inside you are still in love with her and you want to make it work. So you find someone almost exactly like her. You aren't certain if she's the one for you, but instantly you catch feelings.

Everyone catches feelings. It's normal to see someone that you like. I called these *temporary feelings*, because you can only like that person for so long before you realize she is not the right one for you. You don't want to be anyone's rebound. She might be in the same position you're in.

That's why you need to be careful. Don't make any silly decisions that could lead to hurt in the long run. I think men and women make this mistake a lot. In the moment, we get lost and tend to make decisions we end up regretting later. I've done the same things many times. These decisions have really affected me in the long run. It's important to think before you take action.

Feelings aren't permanent, but decisions are. Decisions you make at the end of each relationship should be better, not worse, for the experience. You should not make a decision based on your feelings in the first place, because your feeling likely will not lead to the best thinking. Logic will help a lot to tell you whether you're on the right track.

These situations happen to most people in relationships, and some of them are not happy when they end it. More often than not a person takes instant action based on feelings.

We all have fallen head over heels for another person. You dream about her and see yourself with her for the rest of your lives. Every moment you spend with her feels like heaven on earth. You never want to leave her side.

Then she starts acting funny. Her feelings aren't the same anymore. Don't jump to conclusions and start blaming yourself. I repeat, *do not* blame yourself. She probably caught feelings for somebody else. But those feelings are *only temporary*. She doesn't want to make them permanent, because if she does, she will end up losing you in the process.

Sounds crazy, right? I bet you if you did the same thing to her, she would be upset with you for days or weeks or even months.

Sometimes I don't get people. That's why I always say love is not complicated, people are. All the damn time, finding excuses to do what they want in a relationship when they can be single and never have to explain.

Temporary feelings will only last for so long before you realize what you really want. So don't mess with anyone's feelings if you are unsure of yours.

Feelings are human nature. Sometimes we cannot control how we feel. It's a simple fact that we let our feelings control us and lead us. No one knows how we really feel. Regardless of who we date or who we end up with, we will always have feelings for the a person we were once deeply in love with.

I've been caught up many times catching feeling for random women who weren't worth my time. At that moment, that's how I felt. Can you blame me? I grew up and started to figure things out. I started understanding why I was the way I was. It made me realize that I was worth more than I thought. I wasn't blinded by love anymore. I had a clean slot to do what was right in life. Honestly, I took that chance to change my life.

When you have someone good in your life, never let them go. You will never find that special person again. Expressing feelings for someone who won't be there for the rest of your life is a big mistake. Not only do you catch feelings, but you set yourself up for failure.

Remember, temporary is short-term while permanent is forever! People confuse these two words all the time, which can cause them to get hurt down the road. People will use you as a rebound to get over their exes. Deep down inside, they're still in love with their exes, but most people will never admit it to you.

Breakups are hard to handle, especially if you took years out your life to build a relationship with someone you love. It's hard letting go, but it's a good decision. You have to do what makes you happy at the end of the day. Don't let any man or woman tell you your relationship is not for you. The same people telling you these things are 100 percent miserable and lonely.

You can love someone today and hate them tomorrow. That comes with a relationship. Some of us will go through it and some of us won't. Everyone's relationship is different. I tell people all the time that if you're not ready to move on from your previous relationship, do not go out there and get into another one. It will never work out! Take the time sit down and think about everything that happened in your relationship. Exclude the negative things that brought it to an end. Make a list of pros and cons and the issues that you need to work on. Taking a positive attitude means building a positive relationship next time.

If you've been hurt physically, you need to get out of the relationship. No one should stay with a person who beats them. Get out on the first strike—the second strike could be your life! Domestic violence is the most common reason why women become victims of crime in America. No woman should live in fear for her life. It's not fair, and it's not right. Domestic abuse makes women scared to get into another relationship. It affects their entire lives.

I say to every woman out there, be careful who you date. There are a lot of crazy men who are not looking for relationships. The bottom line is that abusive behavior from your partner is never acceptable. Women deserve to feel valued, respected, and safe.

Get out of a relationship when you notice things aren't the same anymore. Get out when your partner is just not there for you, when things get rocky for more than six months. If the car breaks down and you can't even call on them, because they're too busy partying while you are stressing out. If your partner doesn't help, why be in the relationship in the first place?

Think about yourself and your feelings. You can't blame yourself because you're not as happy as you used to be. That thinking process will get stuck in your head. Move on with your life. The negative thinking won't last forever, but it will remain in your head till you make the final decision.

A sure sign of an unhealthy relationship is when the same problems recur constantly. If y'all took a break from each other for four months, came back together, and had the same problems, that means it's time for you to move on.

Why stay in a relationship with a person who disrespects you and doesn't appreciate your effort? Nothing is free in life. You have to work hard to earn everything. Sometimes couples see things differently— what to expect from each other, what will happen if one gets sick. These things are important in a relationship, because tomorrow is not promised.

How much hurt can you allow someone to give you? Is it worth staying? Is it worth all the pain in the world? You've made all the sacrifices to see that he's happy, but he never sees how hard you're trying. When will you say to yourself, "This is enough. Why should I be treated like this? Where have I gone wrong to be disrespected by the person I love?"

Never feel guilty about how you feel. You know you've tried. You have a boiling point, like everyone else in this world. You'll know when to raise the white flag. It happens to the best of us. At least you have shown you care about your partner and have invited that person into your heart. It takes courage to open up to someone; not everyone has that ability. You never know what lies on the other side of the door. Take a chance and don't regret it. Before you succeed, you have to fail. You live and you learn!

Balancing everything in your life to be with someone will be a headache at first, but it might be worth it when all is said and done. Helping your partner get his life together is important. You want him to be successful with you, make big decisions with you, and approach life with you.

In a relationship, two people need to agree before moving forward. If your partner keeps making decisions behind your back you're not in a good relationship. It's unhealthy if you're not being told about everything. As a partner, you try to balance your time, priorities, wants, needs, and time with your significant other. If that balance is out of whack, make a point of doing the simple things that brought you together in the first place. Don't let your relationship go dry.

The understanding that develops between partners is another reason why people continue to cling to unhealthy relationships. Don't mistake familiarity for understanding. It's rare for someone to take the time to truly understand you as a person. You can date someone for many years and still not know important things about them.

Understanding helps a relationship; it does not ruin it. Understanding strengthens a bond and makes you feel good. Be patience. Take your time with things. If anything is bothering you, let your partner know. Open up about your true feelings, and hopefully down the line you won't regret it.

We all have experienced a bad, unhealthy relationship. There's nothing anyone can do to change that. All we can do is talk to other people who are going through it and give them the best advice we can. People tend to stay in abusive relationships because they have no one else to love. That's a *big mistake*. No matter how much you love your partner, you can't allow him to abuse you.

Independence is one of the greatest things all of us can claim. We work to achieve many things in our lives. If you're not in a relationship, you should be working on yourself before anything else. That means goals, school, work, and your social life. Being single is a great opportunity for you to focus on you. For those coming out of a bad relationship, get your life back together instead of jumping into another bad relationship. You need time to learn from your past, so you won't make those mistakes again in the future.

When Is the Time to Leave the Relationship?

The best time to leave a relationship is when things aren't the same anymore. Everything is done secretly. The person you're with doesn't seem to want anyone to know the two of you are together. You've given up your heart and soul, you've given it your all, maybe you've even tried counseling.

If kids aren't involved, it's better to end things now. You don't have to explain anything that's going on. The best time to break up is when there's no longer any mutual benefit.

Some people may judge a breakup as being selfish, but I disagree. I advise people to find the person or relationship that works for you. Find the connection that gives you what you need. Don't cling to a relationship that causes you dissatisfaction.

We all know someone right now who is in an unhealthy relationship. He or she has put so much into the relationship, and all the options are exhausted. That person is stuck and needs answers. He or she needs someone to sit down with and talk about the relationship.

If you are not happy, do not stay in the relationship, no matter how much you love your partner. You need to love yourself first. If your partner really does love you, then your partner wouldn't be taking you for granted. People use all of their energy and time to make things right, only to find that their partner is not doing the same. Life is too short to play games.

Relationships should enhance your journey. Too many people give up their own journey to take on someone else's. It's better to decide on your own where you're going in life. Then find other people who are on the same path, and see where you fit in. Do a lot of brainstorming to see exactly what you're looking for. When people create goals and standards for their relationships, they end up having more healthy relationships and know when to quickly end the unhealthy ones.

I repeat, for everyone's safety—if you are in an abusive relationship, *get out of it*. You shouldn't be looking on the internet for advice. If someone is putting their hands on you without your consent, in any way whatsoever, you should leave immediately.

Find someone you can trust with your personal life and your secrets. It can be hard to find a person you know that you can trust this way. The next best thing is to trust a total stranger out of nowhere—a professional therapist, a staff member at a shelter, a minister. Find someone to talk to.

No one deserves to be in an abusive or unhealthy relationship. You deserve to be loved, cherished, respected, and appreciated, in every sense of each word. No one should make excuses. There is no excuse in the world for abuse.

I know relationships aren't easy. I know it's hard to walk away from someone you love. But sometimes when you're in love, that's the best thing you can do for your partner!

Most abuse victims blame themselves for what's going on. Abuse is not your fault. The abuser is the one who needs serious help.

Abusers are often involved in drugs and alcohol. You may not know it. Substance abuse can lead to physical abuse. This is something that you as a partner cannot change. It's already too late. It's already time for professional intervention. The best thing you can do right now is walk away and don't look back.

Some people never change. You can't do it for them. They have to want to change and do the work themselves.

Some people never change.

CHAPTER 7

Key Components

Love

L ove is the most natural feeling any human can experience. Love is kind and beautiful. There are a thousand ways to express love. When a person feels love, everything is changed. It gives you a whole new outlook on life. It gives you peace.

To experience the true meaning of love simply means you are blessed. Love is everything it isn't. It's realistically unreal. If you ask ten people what love means, you're guaranteed to get ten different responses.

We're supposed to love not for reasons of reproduction or because it's normal, but because it's already written for us to experience it. Love starts with a good heart and clear vision. It can fail if you feel desperate to experience it. Love will always come to us and leave as well.

Love is a beautiful feeling that has no true meaning. In any given situation, it can turn ugly. No matter how beautiful love may be, it will always leave an impact once it ends. After your heart is broken, you are still able to love. Although you may feel stripped of everything, the ability to love never leaves. True love can be a reality because there is someone in this world for each person created.

Along with love comes freedom—freedom to be yourself and give your ego a rest. Love is one of those feelings in which bliss never ends.

It allows you to feel comfortable with another person, to be a little more receptive to change, and to share yourself.

Love comes with a lot of hope and disappointing reality. The disappointing reality is that love isn't everything it's thought to be. It comes with a lot of heart and thought. You have to allow yourself to be vulnerable and put yourself out there.

I would never advise anyone give up on love, because true love is real. If you find someone who really loves you, then all the changes and second guessing become worth it.

Most relationships fail because men and women allow their egos to become the "pants-wearer." Some people have good intentions but don't know how to put them into perspective. Other people don't know how to love. They feel it's too much work, and they don't want to share their time and space.

In reality, love is what you make of it. Never overthink it or doubt yourself. Everyone is capable of loving someone. It takes little effort to love. Remember: you must love yourself first.

Freedom

Sorry to say, but in a relationship, there is no freedom. I'm not saying you should expect to be suffocated, but do expect to share your time.

There is such a thing as "me" time in a relationship, if the couple manages their time. During the relative freedom of "me" time, you don't get a pass to run rampant and do as you please. You're in a relationship, and you'll have fun in the relationship. It is possible to go out with your girls or guys, have a few drinks, and bring your ass home. There's nothing wrong with having an identity outside of your relationship as long as you never lose yourself. Respect yourself and your relationship, and remain loyal.

Often, relationships fail because of a controlling partner who wants you all to him- or herself. That partner tries to isolate you from the rest of society. A partner like that has insecurities and will make you feel bad about things you want to do.

Relationships also fail because people don't respect their relationships. They feel they can be in a relationship and still act single. Relationships don't go by easy. It takes time and effort to be in one and to make it last. If you feel you want to be in one but don't want to share time with another, then chances are a relationship isn't for you. Another person's feelings are involved. Why would you want to destroy that person's outlook on love and relationships? Why make that person think badly of you?

Make time for yourself, and respect your relationship.

Honesty

Honesty, whether in a relationship or in general, is everything. No one wants to be labeled a liar. In a relationship, honesty matters because your significant other loves you enough to believe in what you say. Not being honest hurts not only you but your relationship. After you've been caught in a lie, there may come a time when you tell the truth and you're not believed.

Honesty leads to trust and loyalty. Dishonesty can only lead you to have a bad relationship. Miscommunication creates barriers that cause your relationship to fall.

Honesty builds good character. You want to be honest in a relationship so that you have a lasting relationship. Honesty leads to so much more. It brings you and your partner closer and gives you hope to become best friends who can talk about anything.

Women want honesty because women need assurance that their relationships are going strong and steady, and that they have good men on their side. Men want honesty in a relationship because they want to know their ladies are loyal to them. When it's all said and done, you want honesty in your relationship because in every relationship you have to map out a foundation. You don't want to map out a foundation with no idea of what you're building.

Loyalty

Loyalty is the most talked-about topic in our generation. It's talked about throughout family life, friendships, and relationships. Relationships need loyalty so that they last. In addition to trust, loyalty is the starter of all relationships. It says, "Hey, I'm ready to be in a committed relationship and stick by your side." Loyalty lets you as well as your partner know the relationship has a chance of lasting. It's the glue of the relationship and bonds you together.

Loyalty not only bonds you, it gives your relationship strength. You know that things are good. Loyalty tells outsiders that there's no chance of them coming between you. Often loyalty in relationships is tested. There's always going to be someone who wants what you have or who wants to make you stray. It's important to remain loyal because nine times out of ten, if you haven't been loyal, you've cheated. Disloyalty is betrayal. For what reasons would you want to betray your love? It isn't worth it.

Trust

The foundation of any relationship is trust. The saying "If you don't have trust, you don't have anything" is true. Without trust you have nothing at all. Trust promotes a healthy relationship.

If you have any doubts about your partner cheating, ask! It's never okay to become a "fatal attraction" to your partner. This goes for guys as well as girls. Women are known to snoop in their guys' phones or accuse their guys of cheating. Going through a phone is a complete turnoff. It's an invasion of privacy, and it isn't fair that you harass your partner in that manner. Guys are just as guilty. Guys usually won't go through their girls' phones, but they will ask friends questions about who their girls befriend on social networks. A jealous friend will tell you what you want to hear in order to tear apart the relationship.

When you love someone, you should trust. It may be hard to trust again after your heart has been broken. You may feel trust isn't worth it, or that heartbreak is going to happen again. You have to trust that this time will be different. You need to let your guard down in order to make things work.

Trust is everything. It's like love. It gives you security in your relationship and makes you feel safe.

When you do have suspicions, approach your partner in a calm manner. Allow your partner to know you're curious without jumping to conclusions right away. See how he or she responds to you, and go from there.

Never get into a relationship in which you feel you can't trust that person or you're too stubborn to try. Check yourself before you point your finger.

Understanding

Understanding comes right along with communication in relationships. To understand your partner, you need to communicate with them. You can't understand them if you don't communicate. Communication in a relationship shows you're comfortable with each other. You need communication to know if you're both on the same page.

Once you build a strong sense of communication, you have a better understanding of the relationship and where you stand. Communication allows both of you to express how you feel or to talk about things that may be bothering you. Once you achieve ongoing communication, understanding will fall right into play.

It takes time to build communication skills. Not everyone has communication skills, and that makes it hard in a relationship. You and your partner both may be stubborn and not willing to communicate. Without communication, there is no understanding, and your relationship won't get anywhere. You need to understand your partner so when things go wrong or there's an argument, you each know where the other is coming from. Once you understand each other, you become a team. You accept that each of you has flaws. But when a test comes, your communication is so strong that there isn't any room for an interruption.

Commitment

Commitment makes relationships last. Commitment is a big step you take in a relationship. It means you're ready to give it your all and be faithful. Commitment has to start with you.

Some people feel they're giving up too much of their freedom and time when they agree to commit. In reality, all it means is that you remain faithful and respect what you have.

Relationships fail for many reasons, one being lack of commitment. It doesn't take a rocket scientist to understand this is something important. This is about determination. You were determined to get in this relationship; now you have to be determined to make it last. Commitment isn't a scary thing. It helps the relationship more than it destroys your freedom. It lets your partner know you're loyal and mature enough to handle a relationship.

Along with commitment comes structure. Relationships need structure in order to grow into much more.

When women think of commitment, they think about their men being honest and loyal to them. For a woman, commitment is a big thing because this may be the guy she marries one day, and she needs to know she has a solid foundation.

Guys don't focus on commitment as much as women do. A guy does want to know he has a girl who's going to go hard with him and ride out. A guy secretly wants his girl to be his best friend.

Once you have commitment in your relationship, you don't need to worry about anything else. Your team of two will lead your love life to victory. You'll be cheering and celebrating forever.

Values

Values are the good faith that was instilled in you as a child. You've been taught to value family, religion, money, friends, education, and yourself. These things become part of you and build your character. When you become an adult, these things still stick with you.

In a relationship, you must value yourself first in order to value your partner. Value is a form of respect. In any relationship, you should respect your mate.

When you have values, you can see the world much more clearly. You're able to respect and appreciate all things. Valuing your relationship is a wonderful feeling. It shows you love and respect your partner. When you value your relationship, it leads to great things. You can have a lasting relationship that turns into marriage if given the chance to bloom.

It's important to value what you have, because it can all be gone in an instant. When relationships end, there's always some sort of regret. You're always going to wonder what would have happened if you had done things differently. Try your best to never take your relationship for granted. Learn to love and appreciate what you have. Value the special bond between you and your partner. All relationships are special and unique. Cherish what you have always. Value life and love.

Before you jump into a new relationship, make sure you are completely over the previous ones.

CHAPTER 8

How to Make Your Relationship Last

The key to every successful relationship is building it brick by brick, from beginning to end. In order for a relationship to last, you need to try new things that will open new doors, new stories, and new life-changing moments. These are things that could help your relationship down the road.

The person who makes the most difference in the relationship is you. If you are serious about your relationship, take charge and lead the way. Make sure you do your part; always do your part.

Starting as friends is one of the best ways to make a relationship last. My advice is to build a best friendship. Think about the things that make your closest friendships irreplaceable. Consider the trust that comes with true intimacy, the willingness to be more open and more passionate, the confidence that the friendship can withstand some conflict.

Happy couples are each other's protectors. They can count on their partners to listen and try to meet their needs. When you're true friends, you acknowledge and respect what the other person is. You don't try to control or change your partner. Every person needs to change themselves.

Not only that, true friendship creates a sense of safety and security. When you're together, you know you're valued for who you are, and you see the value in your partner.

When you've been with someone a while, you become almost a mind reader. You know everything about your partner. It can be a little scary. But each of you will see with your own eyes that you've been paying attention. You have a shared history and inside jokes.

The truth about relationships, in my opinion, is that you never know how strong your relationship is until it's tested. Too often, the stress of a crisis can pull a couple apart. The good news about this is that when you make it through together, you find yourself tighter than ever. Face down a major challenge together and see how far you guys can go. You will never know what's behind the door if you never attempt to open it. If one of you falls, the other should help that one back up, no matter what the situation is. Things happen down the road. That's something you should prepare for.

Relationship is a home, a refuge against outside storms. Like any home, a relationship requires a strong, lasting foundation. To build one, every couple needs to take certain steps that turn "you" and "I" into "we." You may not move through all the steps in order, and you may circle back to complete certain steps again and again and again. But if you make it through them all, you'll be well on your way toward creating a relationship that will shelter you as long as you both shall live.

What makes a true relationship last a lifetime? Loyalty? Yup. Respect? Sure. But a relationship is not just what you have. It's about what you do to make it stronger, safer, more caring, and more committed.

One of the most important things in any relationship is finding a balance between time for two and time for you. When it comes to togetherness, every couple has a unique sweet spot. There are couples who are never apart and there are couples who see each other only on the weekends. Whatever your situation, spending quality time together and valuing every moment should be something that you cherish.

The right balance of time ensures that neither partner feels slighted or smothered. You have shared experiences to fire you up and help you maintain a sense of yourself—not to mention give you something to talk about at the dinner table. But you also have enough time together to feel your connection as a strong tie rather than as a loose thread. Your togetherness needs will also change over time.

In any good relationship, sex is way more than just a physical act. Most of us can't live without it. But people get the wrong ideas about how could sex could save their relationships. Sex does *not* save relationships. It's overrated. Don't let lust determine your faith in a relationship.

What's crucial is the health of your emotional connection. That emotional connection is something only the two of you share. It makes you feel warm and loved. It draws you back together when you're drifting apart.

Things might get rough in the future. Hold down as best you can. Striking up a spark when you first meet is easy. Nurturing a strong, steady flame is the hard part. When you've got a mansion, a potbelly, and a decade of happiness under your belt, it can be hard to muster up the fire you felt when you got first got together That's when it's important to protect your sex life and make it a priority. You to have keep working to create new ways to keep each other happy. Keep revisiting and realizing and reimagining the passion you have for each other. If you keep at it, you'll have a sex life that transcends the lack of newness, the stresses of family and work, and the physical changes that come with aging.

When things go wrong, who's going to be there for you? Who's going be there when you need someone to talk to? If you have someone who's been through everything with you from top to bottom, bottom to top, that's worth holding on to.

Love is the most important ingredient for a relationship. There's so much to learn about another person. There's no "maybe" about love. If you second-guess about loving someone, you do not love that person.

When you love, you enjoy sharing with each other anything and everything. You respect and trust each other. You're always honest with each other. You enjoy spending time and having special moments with each other.

Nothing is more amazing than having someone you can call your own. The good times outnumber the bad times. You're there for each other through it all. You have great conversations. You're close on almost every level. You can balance the time you spend together and the time you spent apart. You would do anything for each other. You protect each other. You're kind to each other. You show affection. You spend time together out of choice, not dependency.

There is always somewhere to go and something to do with each other as date, so when the time comes, be creative. Search for ideas for a beautiful night out. Remember, as partners, basically anywhere you go together and anything you do together is a date. Have fun and build a bond each other. Make Saturday or Friday nights "date nights." Work around your schedules and carve out special time for just you two.

Steps to Making Your Long-Term Relationship Work

- *Communicate about anything and everything*: Have deep feelings and meaningful conversations once in a while. Discuss what's going on in your lives right now, and explain in as much detail as possible, whether the subject is social life, school, work, life, or family life. Learn about each other's pasts. Celebrate accomplishments. Encourage goals and ambitions. Explore other values and beliefs. Share your deepest thoughts, needs, wishes, hopes, and dreams. Know each other inside out.

Don't play games or intentionally act distant to seek control over your partner: This is a form of abuse. You should respect your partner at all times. If your partner speaks to you, reply with compassion, Never stay silent or avoid your partner.

Cooperate: if you don't agree on something, you need to talk about it. There is probably another option. Look for different solutions that you can see eye to eye on. There are many ways to do most things. If we cooperate, the situation will end in the best result for the individuals involved. And, most likely, things will get done faster.

Support each other: Be there for everything. Be there through the good, happy, sad, and bad times, no matter what. Be willing to provide hugs, kisses, and emotional comfort in all circumstances. If your partner resists your attempts, comfort him or her. Ease off the subject and wait until your partner seems to be in a better mood. Create the feeling that you can count on each other.

Never be selfish: If you give nothing of yourself, then you'll get nothing in return. Mean what you say, and say what you mean. Actions speak louder than words.

Be completely honest with each other: An emotionally intimate relationship requires open and honest communication. Keeping secrets from your partner creates a barrier between you and limits emotional trust. Honesty can be scary. But if you want your relationship to thrive, then you both need to become comfortable discussing your feelings, insecurities, and frustrations.

Spend time together: Be independent and keep your sense of self. Never lose yourself or your voice in the relationship. Don't suffocate each other. You should each continue to grow as individuals, not just as a couple. You should have your own space, too—physically and emotionally. Do your own things separately. Just ensure that no other relationship or pursuit crowds out your partner from being your priority.

Decide to love: Infatuation is typically what sparks loving relationships, but the excitement fades. Warm feelings diminish unless both partners make conscious efforts to uphold their companionship. Once love is established, actively expressing love will maintain and increase the loving feelings in both partners. Conversely, refraining from expressions of love allows one's devotion to dissipate. If you are aiming for a long-lasting, successful relationship, you need to commit to your partner's emotional well-being, even when it isn't easy.

Nothing is perfect in this world. Nothing happens overnight. If you want to have a decent or great relationship, you have to work on it. My beautiful girlfriend broke down what love and relationships really mean to her: "A relationship is a team connection between two people. They share a bond. They have a commitment. They tolerate and work through their differences. They know how to compromise to make each other happy.

"A relationship is translucent. Nothing is kept hidden. It's knowing that, regardless of the situation, one will never have to face it alone. Love is letting go—being completely vulnerable and open, and having honesty, trust, comfort, and compassion. It's wanting to put someone else's needs before your own, but not leaving yourself out in the cold. It's being nurturing and stable. It's being able to go through hell and back with that person right by your side. It's being able to see your partner's flaws and still love him or her exactly the same. Instead of running from your partner's weakness, you run toward your partner.

"Love is being motivational and uplifting. It's only wanting the best for each other."

Everybody has their own definitions of what the words love and relationship mean to them. What do those words mean to you? Take time to reflect on it.

The key to success: invest now, spend later!

CHAPTER 9

The Spoken Truth

I decided to write a book called *The Spoken Truth* to express my thoughts about heartbroken women, about my generation, and about relationships. I realize that people have lost their morals about relationships. It seems to me that you have to give in order to receive back. I'm not saying you shouldn't give at all; I'm saying you should give the same treatment you receive. It's only right.

People don't care anymore. If you're not taking them shopping or to a fancy restaurant, if you're not spending any type of money on them, they'll find a way to get that from somebody else. But from my point of view, when you're in love with someone, those things don't matter. What matters is keeping each other happy.

So many things have changed in our community and our world. We can't point fingers or blame anybody else for our mistakes. We should point the fingers at ourselves.

I took the time to research and understand why men continue to hurt all these good women. The simple fact is these men have never had a *real* woman in their lives. They were always chasing the wrong type of women, who screw them over at the end. When a man like this meets a good woman who's willing to give him the world, he decides to screw her over, thinking she'll hurt him too.

Some men express negative feelings because we keep getting hurt. I can't blame the good women because they haven't done anything wrong. Men just have to take their sweet time and get to know a real woman before expecting anything out of her.

A real woman is hard to come by; so is a good man. People sometimes expect a lot from one person when that person doesn't expect anything from them. People can be ungrateful even when they are treated right. They take advantage every chance that they get.

It's sad when people stay committed to the wrong partners. I hope my book can change people's views on love and change the way they treat other people. All these good, smart, beautiful, independent women deserve to be treated like queens every single second of every day. If she's giving you her all, if she's holding you down 24/7, if she's making sure you stay on top of your goals, if she's trying to keep you happy—you better see that. If you don't see that, that's means you never deserved her from the start. Cherish what you have or watch the next person cherish it for you.

I hope when readers finish my book, they've gotten some of the answers they were looking for. So many people get stuck on step one and never figure it out after that. I did not write this book to show everyone I know everything about relationships. I wrote this book because I've been through it. After the experiences I've had, I don't want anyone else to go through it!

Many people come to a breaking point where they can no longer see themselves in a relationship. I can't blame people for that—there's too many mind games! To be happy in any type of relationship, you need to be happy with yourself first. That's the most important thing. People forget what's important to them. They miss out on a lot of stuff they won't see again.

Be honest at all times. Be nice about it, but be honest, especially to the person you get involved with. Trust is gained through honesty. Don't ever forget to be honest with yourself too, because to be honest with another, you must first accept the truth.

Any relationship you get into won't be easy. You'll argue. Get prepared and be ready to hold it down the best way you can. If it doesn't happen the way you want it to, at least you'll know you tried your best.

It's healthy to tell the world how much you guys love each other. It's not healthy to have a screaming match in front of others. That just shows that you'd rather argue than love. Nor is it okay to fight behind closed doors. Do what's best for the relationship and keep it healthy. Sit down with each other. Discuss the issues; don't scream about them. We all know in every relationship there is a fight at some point. Even the president and the First Lady have their differences, but we will never know what those are because they keep their business to themselves. That's how it should be.

Falling in love takes time and patience. Let's say you fall in love with a person, and the person don't feel the same way about you because of trust or some other major, internal issue. It's not your job to fix the person you love. You can't force another person to love you. You cannot fix another person. But you can help other people to fix themselves. Maybe, down the road, the person you love can see what type of person you are, that you're not like everyone else who's trying to hurt them.

Every life journey goes through a whole lot of interesting things. Some would surprise you. You can't resolve or control these things. All you can do is be the person who stuck around through the ups and the downs. Just be there and help the one you love get through it. Getting frustrated about things won't help your relationship get better.

People are afraid to love, care, and trust again after being hurt. This could be because they don't have the right person telling them that love still exists. The right person will be showing it! Who wants to be alone and be miserable for the rest of their lives? Think about it. We've all had bad experiences. We've dealt with a lot of bullshit. We've been through it all. That comes with any relationship.

The simple fact that we go through what we go through shows us that all relationships weren't meant to be. When things come to end, it doesn't mean the end of the world. It means you can go out and find someone else who's right for you. There is someone out there who reaches your standards, who can treat you well, who can be by your side when things get rough, who can love you the way you love them. It's rare to find these things; that's the society we're living in today.

Don't get me wrong, I had to learn on my own that anything is possible. Just never doubt that it's true. I want people to tell me that *The Spoken Truth* helped their relationships or made them set standards so they won't settle for less in their next relationship.

There's so much to learn from an individual once you start talking. It takes time and trust for a person to want to open up. It's very important—I'm going to say it again—it's *very* important to recognize the person you're with has not always been that person. Your partner has gone through things to make him or her into the person you see now. Someone probably took your partner's love and money for granted. You will never know until he or she opens up and tells you.

Appreciate your partner's past fully to understand what he or she is really going through. You can give your input and help change things down the road. This will help your relationship, make you a better person, and show your partner that you really care.

Put your partner at ease. Maybe he or she doesn't express feelings well because the family is not particularly expressive. Maybe she or he is insecure because an ex was very critical. Be conscious of these things. Anything that you do has an impact on your partner as well.

Be careful who you talk to, hang with, and tell your business to. Rumors can spread the same night, and always get back to the person you're with. Keep each other happy. Don't let anyone else in your business. Don't let anyone, and I mean *anyone*, steal the happiness you work so hard for.

Look at the people around you and tell me how many are actually happy with their love lives. Not many. People pretend to be happy when in reality they really are not. Most of your so-called friends would be happy if you were not in a relationship, because they see how happy you are and envy you. It gets them mad because they can't have it.

Character plays a major role for everyone. The smallest things can trigger the biggest problems. That's what matters most to women—the small things. No matter how mad she is with you, she will always remember the small things you've done for her. Men need to understand women more, especially women's emotions. Women take their emotions very seriously, as should men. Be careful what you say to women, because women never forget what you say. Don't make empty promises.

Everyone who's currently in a relationship should value it at all times. Tons of couples forget each other's interests, and that's when things start going downhill. If you have different interests, which is perfectly fine, make sure you value what your partner's interests are. It just might interest you down the line; you never know unless you give it a try. Sometimes you need to stop being selfish and try new things. It won't hurt you. But it will show your partner that you care about what he or she cares about. Do your best to pay attention and have respect for what your partner likes. All things come with love.

No one is perfect. If you think you can find the perfect "one," be my guest and travel the world. You won't find what you're looking for. There's no perfect person, no perfect relationship, no perfect world. Everyone comes with flaws, broken hearts, and trust issues. We all have a past. If you can't see yourself with someone because that person has a past, you're not ready for a relationship. You have a lot of growing up to do.

Writing The Spoken Truth has taught me about myself. I've revealed so much to you guys. I am happy and pleased that I wrote this book. I hope it will help people make smarter decisions. I hope everyone who reads it can apply it to current and future relationships. Above all, you don't want to waste your time. Every single day of your life counts. If I've helped you in any way, my goal is accomplished.

Make your own love story. Remember that true love occurs only if you believe in yourself, the person you're with, and the relationship. Thank you!

Printed in the United States
By Bookmasters